The Object Lessons series achieves something very close to magic: the books take ordinary—even banal—objects and animate them with a rich history of invention, political struggle, science, and popular mythology. Filled with fascinating details and conveyed in sharp, accessible prose, the books make the everyday world come to life. Be warned: once you've read a few of these, you'll start walking around your house, picking up random objects, and musing aloud: 'I wonder what the story is behind this thing?'"

Steven Johnson, author of *Where Good Ideas Come From* and *How We Got to Now*

Object Lessons describe themselves as 'short, beautiful books,' and to that, I'll say, amen. . . . If you read enough Object Lessons books, you'll fill your head with plenty of trivia to amaze and annoy your friends and loved ones—caution recommended on pontificating on the objects surrounding you. More importantly, though . . . they inspire us to take a second look at parts of the everyday that we've taken for granted. These are not so much lessons about the objects themselves, but opportunities for self-reflection and storytelling. They remind us that we are surrounded by a wondrous world, as long as we care to look."

John Warner, *The Chicago Tribune*

T0347587

The joy of the series, of reading *Remote Control, Golf Ball, Driver's License, Drone, Silence, Glass, Refrigerator, Hotel*, and *Waste* . . . in quick succession, lies in encountering the various turns through which each of their authors has been put by his or her object. . . . The object predominates, sits squarely center stage, directs the action. The object decides the genre, the chronology, and the limits of the study. Accordingly, the author has to take her cue from the *thing* she chose or that chose her. The result is a wonderfully uneven series of books, each one a *thing* unto itself."

Julian Yates, *Los Angeles Review of Books*

The Object Lessons series has a beautifully simple premise. Each book or essay centers on a specific object. This can be mundane or unexpected, humorous or politically timely. Whatever the subject, these descriptions reveal the rich worlds hidden under the surface of things."

Christine Ro, *Book Riot*

. . . a sensibility somewhere between Roland Barthes and Wes Anderson."

Simon Reynolds, author of *Retromania: Pop Culture's Addiction to Its Own Past*

OBJECTLESSONS

A book series about the hidden lives of ordinary things.

Series Editors:

Ian Bogost and Christopher Schaberg

Advisory Board:

Sara Ahmed, Jane Bennett, Jeffrey Jerome Cohen, Johanna Drucker, Raiford Guins, Graham Harman, renée hoogland, Pam Houston, Eileen Joy, Douglas Kahn, Daniel Miller, Esther Milne, Timothy Morton, Kathleen Stewart, Nigel Thrift, Rob Walker, Michele White.

In association with

BOOKS IN THE SERIES

glitter

NICOLE SEYMOUR

BLOOMSBURY ACADEMIC
NEW YORK • LONDON • OXFORD • NEW DELHI • SYDNEY

BLOOMSBURY ACADEMIC
Bloomsbury Publishing Inc
1385 Broadway, New York, NY 10018, USA
50 Bedford Square, London, WC1B 3DP, UK
29 Earlsfort Terrace, Dublin 2, Ireland

BLOOMSBURY, BLOOMSBURY ACADEMIC and the Diana logo are trademarks
of Bloomsbury Publishing Plc

First published in the United States of America 2022

Copyright © Nicole Seymour, 2022

Cover design: Alice Marwick

Epigraph by Maria Sledmere from "Whitechapel" used by permission of
the author. All Rights Reserved

Library of Congress Cataloging-in-Publication Data
Names: Seymour, Nicole, author.
Title: Glitter / Nicole Seymour.
Description: New York, NY: Bloomsbury Academic, 2022. | Series: Object lessons |
Includes bibliographical references and index. | Summary: From Cleopatra to Coachella,
this book tracks the enduring, emotionally-charged human relationship to glitter-a variously-
composed object that reveals the gendered and sexualized ways we interact with our
environment and respond to its crises"– Provided by publisher.
Identifiers: LCCN 2021051810 (print) | LCCN 2021051811 (ebook) | ISBN 9781501373763
(paperback) | ISBN 9781501373770 (epub) | ISBN 9781501373787 (pdf) | ISBN 9781501373794
Subjects: LCSH: Decoration and ornament–Psychological aspects. | Glitter art. |
Pollution prevention.
Classification: LCC NK1505 .S39 2022 (print) | LCC NK1505 (ebook) |
DDC 745.4–dc23/eng/20220105
LC record available at https://lccn.loc.gov/2021051810
LC ebook record available at https://lccn.loc.gov/2021051811

ISBN: PB: 978-1-5013-7376-3
ePDF: 978-1-5013-7378-7
eBook: 978-15013-7377-0

Series: Object Lessons

Typeset by Deanta Global Publishing Services, Chennai, India
Printed and bound in the United States of America

To find out more about our authors and books visit www.bloomsbury.com
and sign up for our newsletters.

Now that glitter is cancelled

I can write my *Object Lessons* book

on the sparkle emoji

and call it lit.

—Maria Sledmere, "Whitechapel"

CONTENTS

Diary Entry: Glitter in Quarantine

It's mid-March, 2020 and I am trying to make a mask out of a bandana and two hair ties, following the viral video that many of you no doubt watched. I open the medicine cabinet to retrieve the hair ties, but then realize that I haven't cleaned the cabinet knob recently. So I use a disinfectant wipe to clean it and then open the cabinet. But then I realize that I didn't wash my hands after touching the possibly unclean knob. So I wash my hands, clean the knob again, wash my hands again, touch the knob, and finally open the cabinet to get the hair ties. The rest of the day proceeds like this, at once terrifying and comically repetitive, like some kind of silent film short.

Around this same time, UNICEF releases a document titled, "How Teachers Can Talk to Children about Coronavirus Disease (COVID-19)." It urges those who work with primary school students to "[d]emonstrate why it's so important to wash hands for 20 seconds with soap. For example, put a small amount of glitter in a student's hands and have them wash them with just water and notice how much glitter remains. Then have them wash for 20 seconds with soap and water and see how the glitter is gone."[1]

Others are more pessimistic about the possibility of ridding oneself of glitter and/or germs. A Facebook post and Tweet from an Australian doctor named Ken McGrath goes viral around this time, asking, "Have you ever . . . hugged or shaken hands with someone who was wearing or using [glitter]? And for the next two weeks, it hangs around forever [*sic*] and ends up on surfaces you can't recall touching, even after showering & washing?" After a space, McGrath delivers his punchline: "Think of COVID-19 as glitter."[2]

I find myself wishing that the coronavirus were in fact *more* like glitter—visible, unmistakable. Instead, I am wracked with paranoia as I imagine myself surrounded by the invisible traces of a virus that, at this moment, we know so little about.

Of course, the analogy between glitter and germs or disease is not new. I recall Demetri Martin's famous (and admittedly funny) joke that "glitter is the herpes of craft supplies."[3] And how, pre-Covid, the National Education Association suggested the same basic lesson as UNICEF on a now-defunct Web page titled "Glitter Germs." As they affirmed, "The point really gets across and the kids love it!" Here, glitter is simultaneously toxic and enticing—a love/hate paradigm that this book will trace extensively. Indeed, one wonders how, exactly, something so lovable to children can stoke their fear of the virus or bacteria it stands in for. On the other hand, as we will see later in this book, so-called "glitterbombers" harness a certain anxiety of contagion in their innovative uses of this substance.

One could say that glitter has been its own kind of sparkly plague to me as well. For years I have not been able to shake it; for years I've been trying to write this book. But at the same time that it has clung to me and caught me, glitter has also defied my conceptual grasp, just as McGrath suggests it defies our literal grasp—and, as I will show, that of forces ranging from washing machine filters to film animators.

An irony, then: glitter captures us, our attention, our glance, the light, but *we* cannot capture *it*. How to even try? To isolate one or two pieces by anecdote or case study would seem to fail to capture the essence of the whole—the way that one can only have glitter in the plural, and never *a* glitter. But perhaps, in dazzling you with a few of its facets, the chapters you find here can add up to something that feels like a whole. This book, then, is paradoxically dedicated to the art of trying to pin down something that eludes capture.

1 THE GREAT GLITTER BACKLASH

"What decorates? And how? Why should the ecologically minded practitioner of the humanities concern herself with decorating—an activity of expenditure, of waste?"

—DANIEL C. REMEIN[1]

In December 2017, I volunteered for a beach cleanup in my hometown of Long Beach, California, organized by the anti-plastic pollution organization Algalita. As my shift was ending, I discovered a patch of sparkly, colorful glitter scattered behind some rocks. It was undeniably beautiful—especially compared to the drab cigarette butts, plastic bottle caps, plastic straws, and shards of Styrofoam I had been gathering up until then. I felt strangely protective of this substance, as if I had discovered a hidden stockpile of precious gems. Knowing that I would never be able to clean it all up—and that I would pick up more sand than glitter trying—I left it there.

No doubt I was thinking at that moment of a particular news story that had started circulating in the UK and US media about a month prior. The story goes something like this: glitter consists of nonbiodegradable microplastics (pieces less than 5 mm in diameter) and therefore pollutes the environment, especially the ocean. This type of glitter, along with myriad other microplastics, gets washed down sink or shower drains or escapes the filters of washing machines. Then, since "the ocean is downhill from nearly everywhere, drainage systems for cities and towns typically lead to rivers that, however circuitously, eventually empty into the ocean," according to Captain Charles Moore—who happens to be Algalita's founder as well as the person who first discovered the so-called Great Pacific Garbage Patch.[2] In the ocean, microplastics can both absorb and release chemicals, while plankton, fish that eat plankton, and other organisms can ingest those particles. Subsequently, depending on our dietary habits, some of us may consume said fish. While the ultimate consequences of microplastic pollution are still unknown, it does not bode particularly well for the health of aquatic ecosystems, nor that of humans.[3]

In light of these trajectories and their possible risks, New Zealand environmental anthropologist Trisia Farrelly initially sounded the alarm: "I think all glitter should be banned because it's microplastic," she told media outlets on November 16, 2017.[4] The headlines proliferated. For example,

CNN soon reported that "Glitter Is Not Just Annoying, It Could Be Bad for the Environment," while a not-so-subtle *Newsweek* piece blared, "Glitter Is an Environmental Scourge That Is Wrecking the Oceans. Should It Be Banned?"[5] This news story seemed to take on qualities of glitter itself: it was ubiquitous and inescapable.

And in fact, this backlash has resurfaced like clockwork for the past four seasons since—perhaps in anticipation of the winter holidays and the glittery cards, decorations, and wrapping paper they usher in. In December 2018, for example, an academic I greatly admire Tweeted, "Glitter is a microplastic that takes over 1,000 years to degrade and is harmful to aquatic life. Happy holidays."[6] And in October 2020, an article in *The Guardian* thundered, "Glitter Is an Environmental Abomination. It's Time to Stop Using It."[7]

They have a point. After all, the beach cleanup was not the first time I have discovered such a substance in a "natural" context—not surprising, given that microplastics are the most plentiful form of solid waste on the planet.[8] While walking around the University of California, Riverside's arboretum in May 2019, I saw a sign urging graduates not to "throw glitter or fairy dust [during celebrations or photo ops] as this is a potential hazard to wildlife"—right *after* I saw small silver pieces of plastic shaped like mortarboard caps on the ground. (Unbelievably, but truly, I was on campus to give a talk on glitter.)

But I think this glitter backlash deserves some scrutiny. For one thing, despite Farrelly's rather matter-of-fact statement, not all glitter is microplastic—an important point that I will explore in Chapter 4. And, as it turns out, glitter does not actually seem to be a major source of microplastic pollution. A BBC segment estimates that it constitutes maybe .1%—at most—of the overall total in the ocean, with scientists reporting little evidence of significant hazardousness.[9] The vast majority of microplastics in the ocean come from materials such as car tires and synthetic textiles used in clothing.[10]

It's also worth noting at this point that the plastic glitter with which many of us are familiar initially came from recycled materials. US machinist Harry Ruschmann apparently invented the first commercial glitter product in 1934 as a means of disposing of scrap plastics.[11] (Today, his Meadowbrook Inventions company still thrives, calling itself "the world's leading Glitter manufacturer, Glitter supplier, and Glitter distributor.") And plastic itself emerged as a recycled material: When industrialist John D. Rockefeller witnessed his oil refineries burning off ethylene gas, he reportedly declared, "'I don't believe in waste . . . Figure out something to do with it.' That 'something' turned out to be polyethylene," the most commonly-used plastic today.[12] So even if we do think of glitter as plastic—which, yet again, is only part of the story—and of plastic as wasteful and hazardous, its origins lie in impulses toward (capitalist) efficiency and usefulness.

While such facts simply went unmentioned in much of the media coverage, other accounts could be accused of confusing the public and conflating glitter with microplastics.

A 2018 *Independent* article reports that the "Drastic on Plastic" initiative in the UK "will outlaw that festival favorite: glitter"—but then later explains that "all traders . . . must use biodegradable glitter."[13] A December 2019 *Daily Mail* article on the subject began with bullet pointed-sentences including, "Glitter is made of a microplastic known as Mylar, which is hurting ocean life. This plastic accounts for 92.4% of the 5.25 trillion pieces of plastic in the ocean." The ambiguous phrase "This plastic" refers to Mylar, though one could easily read it as referring to glitter. Further confusing the issue, Mylar is a specific brand name for the generic substance polyethylene terephthalate, or PET—used in countless products from peanut butter jars to tennis balls.[14] And yet I have heard no outrage over the use of bread spreads, nor any calls to cancel Wimbledon. So why has glitter become such a cultural punching bag?

Glitter as Scapegoat, Part I

There are multiple possible answers to that question. Perhaps the most obvious is that this particular narrative—that something seemingly frivolous, fun, playful, miniscule, and delightful, at least to some, could turn out to be an environmental "scourge" or "abomination"—fits the demands of our clickbait-driven, 24-hour news cycle. (I'm actually surprised that journalists didn't use formulations in their headlines such as, "You'll Never Believe These Terrible

Facts about Glitter!" or, "The Truth about Glitter That the Craft and Cosmetic Industries Don't Want You to Know!")

Another possible answer is that the "glitter-is-bad-for-the-environment" narrative snaps easily into the well-worn groove that I've come to call "killjoy environmentalism." I have dedicated much of my academic career to studying the dominance as well as the hazards of the relentless "doom and gloom," self-righteousness, and shaming found in environmental art, activism, and discourse. As I have outlined, these modes can lead to fatigue and even denialism on the part of the public. And yet they persist. The preachy, finger-wagging, killjoy environmentalist has actually become a cultural cliché, thanks to popular representations such as Lisa Simpson on the classic animated TV show *The Simpsons*. In that sense, this news story is not particularly shocking, insofar as it fits the apocalyptic script in which every conceivable behavior or product is bad for the environment. Happy holidays, indeed.

Which brings us to the point that the facts about glitter are perhaps less important, or at least less interesting, than the *feelings* this substance inspires. Consider how this news story seemed to have a cathartic function, as countless individuals on the Internet revealed their passionate loathing—and, to a lesser extent, passionate defenses—of glitter. Some educational institutions, supermarkets, and department stores have operationalized this loathing by instituting the bans Farrelly called for.[15] One nursery school in the UK, for example, reported that they swapped craft glitter out for the notably drabber media of lentils and rice.[16] Here, we might wonder if the glitter backlash can, in part, be explained through the concept of "greenwashing"—because if a supermarket chain such as Waitrose can say they've banned glitter (which they have, kind of[17]), they can distract us from the zillions of *other* plastic items they still sell.

Meanwhile, glitter products continue to proliferate and diversify, suggesting that consumer enthusiasm for this substance is far from waning. Today you can procure everything from glitter sunscreen (which I personally can't recommend unless you want to be coated in a chalky white film flecked with sparkles) to glitter coffins (I'm currently saving up for mine).[18] As blogger Penny Whitehouse sums up the bigger picture: "Glitter. You either love it or hate it, right?"[19] This love-hate dynamic is one of the major threads that runs throughout this book. In what follows, I will take a closer look at the powerful and often unexamined emotional investments and unconscious cultural connotations we hold in relation to glitter.

And in fact, we could identify some cultural prejudices lurking below the surface of the Great Glitter Backlash, considering that glitter is typically associated with marginalized identities and subject positions including children, girls, women, feminine people, drag performers, queer people, transgender people, and people of color—categories that, of course, overlap in various ways. ("Queer" is a shorthand that I'll use throughout this book to refer to lesbian, gay, bisexual, transgender, and other non-dominant sexual and gender identities.) These identities and subject positions have been devalued, ridiculed, and treated as unpolitical or unimportant in mainstream Western cultures. And more specifically, they have been associated with devalued conceptual categories such as frivolity, "waste," and aesthetics (art, indulgence) over ascetics (austerity, self-discipline). Let's explore some of those cultural connections—primarily, those of queer people and people of color—before returning to the question of prejudices.

"Glitter and Be Gay": Glitter's Queer Connections

Performance theorist Katie Schaag informs us that "queer aesthetics, from camp cinema to non-binary fashion, rely upon plastic materials such as glitter, silicone, and spandex, as well as plastic-inflected visuals."[20] (However, as I am suggesting, *alternatives* to plastic glitter are plentiful.) Drag performers in particular are known for their love of glitter— as indicated by a recent *Glamour* magazine roundtable that asked several queens to rate the best cosmetic glitter products.[21] In short, glitter often serves as a tool to blur gender lines.

To understand these gender-bending dynamics in a bit more depth, let's turn to an historical example: the UK and US musical movement of the early 1970s known as glam rock or, sometimes, glitter rock. Artists such as David Bowie, Jobriath, Slade, The Sweet, and my personal, underrated fave,

T. Rex, eschewed the more natural hippie look that was also popular at the time, donning sparkly or shiny cognates such as sequins, satin, silk and its variations such as chiffon and taffeta, velvet, brocade, lamé, or Lurex. These predominantly male artists also embraced recent trends in women's makeup; 1967 had been the "year for glitter and glint," when "'gleamiest gold-gold'" eyeshadows, lipsticks marketed with copy such as "'Silver Rage!' and 'Gold Rage!,'" and even rhinestone-encrusted false eyelashes hit the market.[22] Media scholar Julia Leyda explains that "part of the shock value of glam rock lay in its overt rejection of essentialized gender and sexual categories—the boy and girl fans wore long hair, makeup and platform shoes, while the (mostly) male stars flaunted their bisexuality on stage and in the press."[23] Or, as Bowie put it more simply in his 1974 hit "Rebel Rebel": "Got your mother in a whirl cuz she's/Not sure if you're a boy or a girl."[24]

My mother delivered me, as a girl, 5 years after that tune hit the airwaves. By age 13 I worshipped David Bowie, enthusiastically plunging both her and my father into a whirl. (I would say that, at this time, I thought of Bowie and myself as being the same gender. Perhaps I still do.) I shaved my head and sported silver glitter gel in the spiky remainders, along with black lipstick, a black skirt criss-crossed with sparkly silver stitching, silver 20-hole Doc Martens boots, and a red satin jacket that I bought at the Goodwill. I fell asleep every night looking at a vintage picture on my wall of Bowie onstage in a silver quilted suit, simulating fellatio on his guitarist Mick Ronson, who was clad in a satin bomber jacket and matching pants. When the glam rock revival hit, I was ready—hunting down import vinyl records from The London Suede at Pier Records in Newport Beach, California and obsessively rewatching Todd Haynes' *Velvet Goldmine* (1998). The latter, a filmic homage to glam/glitter rock named after a Bowie song, recreates the aforementioned fellatio scene and also features another in which bisexual musician Curt Wild (Ewan McGregor, playing a composite of Iggy Pop and Lou Reed) shakes a can of loose glitter in front of his crotch while on stage, mimicking ejaculation.

Considering how glitter enables slides across gender categories, we could also think of it as specifically transgender, not just queer. In fact, transgender studies scholar Z Nicolazzo has quipped, "When we come out as trans, we don't get a free t-shirt in the mail; we do, however, get a package of glitter."[25] Of course, we must note here that shiny and sparkly accoutrement—and aesthetic opulence more generally—were historically, and normatively, linked to straight cisgender men throughout European history. But "after the storming of the Bastille in 1789 Paris, anything resembling royalty or excess was no longer en vogue."[26] We should also acknowledge that, today, glitter is most often linked to feminine cisgender gay men and straight cisgender women. As student Leonie Müller pointed out to me, that link replicates the real-life scenarios in which queer women, especially masculine queer women, have comparatively less cultural visibility. Even so, glitter's applications can vary widely, and to great effect. One anonymous queer female blogger, in a piece whose title bluntly states the point I hope to make a little more subtly here—"Glitter Hate is Homophobia"—describes how "glitter spread on top of my butchness [makes] people uncomfortable. If there's something that elicits more gender panic than inversion, it's high contrast: . . . high heels on someone with a beard, glitter on an unwashed punk."[27]

More than a material resource for queer communities and individuals, glitter has also served to symbolize or signal queerness, as with the widely-circulated statement attributed to Lady Gaga: "Being gay is like glitter; it never goes away." Even the verb form of the word has served similar functions. In 1956, closeted composer Leonard Bernstein debuted the operetta *Candide*, based on Voltaire's novella of the same name, featuring an aria with the suggestive title, "Glitter and Be Gay."[28] And then there's the unsubtle newspaper headline in *Velvet Goldmine* after singer Brian Slade announces his bisexuality in a press conference: "All That Glitters Is— Gay!!!"

But these cultural associations run so deep that sometimes one doesn't even need to spell them out. Just a few days before the aforementioned beach cleanup, I was listening to National Public Radio's quiz show *Wait Wait . . . Don't Tell Me!* when, following a segment about the glitter backlash, host Peter Sagal joked that "[g]litter pollution has gotten so bad, some researchers say that by 2025, a full two thirds of ocean life will look *faaabulous*"—the latter word delivered in an unmistakably fey tone that implies the glitter/queerness connection.[29]

Being Seen: Glitter, Race, and Ethnicity

Glitter is not as closely tied to (queer) people of color in the public imagination as it is to (white) queer people. Even so, recent media have invited us to consider this intersection. Let's turn to the case of BioGlitz, a biodegradable glitter brand I examine in depth in Chapter 4. BioGlitz employs racially diverse models and appeals to consumers concerned with inclusion and social justice; their social media hashtag is #glitzforall, while another slogan reads, "Supporting all colors." Such phrases seem to speak to both sexuality and race; "all colors" invokes the idea of all the colors of the rainbow and, thus, both the multi-colored LGBTQ+ Pride flag and the wide range of skin tones in the world.

And in fact, glitter seems to blur racial lines as well as gender lines in the BioGlitz universe. In a 2018 photoshoot by Dylan Thomas for *Paper* magazine, models identified as Mantra, Yeera, and Slater are not just gender-ambiguous but also racially ambiguous as they huddle together, covered head to toe in colorful hues of copper, purple, and blue. Similarly, in the short film released by the brand in 2019 in honor of Earth Day, a Black woman gets covered completely in silver glitter.

Some might be skeptical of Bioglitz's glossy (or glossed-over?) visions of post-racial harmony, wherein glitter seems to negate individual differences. But elsewhere, glitter has served more pointedly to navigate issues of race, including as it intersects with gender and sexuality. Quil Lemons, a young Black, queer photographer from the US, focuses on young Black men and men of color for his *GLITTERBOY* photo series, wherein subjects appear with glitter smudged on their cheeks and foreheads. As he observes, "there's a privilege that comes along with being white when it comes to self-expression, sexuality, and fluidity. Black men really don't have that . . . so this project was [designed] to bring light to boys that get overlooked."[30] This statement resonates with art historian Krista Thompson's description of how "photography privileges whiteness": not just in the sense that, historically, only white people have been deemed worthy of representation, but also in terms of how actual photographic technologies render Black people illegible.[31] Glitter, a substance that typically reflects light, is a small tool with which to change these circumstances.[32] Lemons' series reworks the visual and chromatic lexicon of status, not just in terms of skin color but also in terms of adornment.

Similarly, artist Sadie Barnette created a "glittering bar structure" in 2019 to commemorate the first, but frequently forgotten, Black-owned gay bar in the city of San Francisco, which her father operated in the early 1990s as a "space for folks to shine."[33] Her artist's statement on this mobile installation, *The New Eagle Creek Saloon*, picks up on Lemons' notion of light: "Throughout the installation light radiates, refracted from holographic lounge seating to sparkle stereo equipment to the incandescence of the 'Eagle Creek' neon sign—all suggesting a shimmer between disco and mirage."[34] Here, glitter and its cognates (holography, sparkle, neon, shimmer) highlight both a forgotten past ("disco," in shorthand) and a possible future ("mirage"). While shimmery, glittering things were once the provenance of the privileged, artists like Lemons and Barnette use glitter to bring attention to marginalized groups that have been denied the literal and figurative spotlight for far too long. And indeed, we could place their work within longer aesthetic traditions—linking them, for example, to 1920s-era blues singer Ma Rainey, who "flamboyantly adorned her outfits with 'sequins, beads, rhinestones, gold, and ostrich feathers . . . a queen's wardrobe of glimmer and shine' . . . as a way to claim racial equality."[35]

Glitter, shimmer, and shine might also serve as means for marginalized racial and ethnic groups to process the cultural stereotypes placed upon them. Consider tRASHY Clothing, a "satirical rtw [ready to wear] label from Palestine & the Arab world."[36] One of their Instagram posts features a male model wearing a bright blue *galabeya*, the round-necked, long-sleeved garment found commonly on men throughout the Middle East—though typically in more low-key colors—splayed out in front of tapestries and pillows embroidered with *terter*, a local term for glittery thread or sequins."[37] Scholar Aya El Sharkawy categorizes such images as "Arab Camp": they lampoon the long tradition of Western culturemakers exoticizing and fetishizing "the Orient," and counter the widespread assumption that this geographic region lacks queer culture or sensibility.[38]

Glitter as Scapegoat, Part II

If glitter is connected materially and metaphorically to queerness and related categories such as femininity, and if it has recently been mobilized by artists of color to redress past and ongoing harms, then stigmatizing this substance has discriminatory implications. To paraphrase my student Jose Arriola after I described this book project to my queer literature class, if the attack on glitter is anything more than just clickbait to sell ads, it's as much about minority cultures as it is about plastic.

But how do these discriminatory implications work, exactly? Let's back up. Recall the epigraph from Daniel Remein at the top of this chapter, which alludes to the dominant association between decoration and waste. Glitter is decorative and not functional in any significant way, so from the start it occupies the category of waste in the cultural imagination—both in the noun sense of "trash" and in the verb sense of "destroy" or "squander." Meanwhile, those who love this substance—women, queer people, children, etc.—are also frequently perceived as wasteful or trashy, not to mention frivolous, indulgent, messy, playful, emotional, and disgusting.[39]

For instance, feminist scholars have shown that biological processes typically correlated to women, such as menstruation, are perceived as wasteful and disgusting[40]—to say nothing of the fact that women are the target customers for arguably unnecessary products such as jewelry and cosmetics. When it comes to queer people, Vanbasten Noronha de Araújo explains that "the queer body is . . . equated with unproductivity and non-reproductivity," largely for its failure to fit into what have been deemed as natural patterns of impregnation and/or childbearing.[41] Queer ecology scholar Robert Azzarello has more specifically demonstrated how associations around queerness can feed into environmentalist thinking in problematic ways, thus combining the potent forces of sexual shame and environmental shame. As he points out, "the most popular terms to describe environmental crisis—unnatural, diseased, pathological, risky, contaminated, suicidal, and so on—are exactly those terms that have been used historically to stigmatize sexual misfits."[42]

Extending such thinking, I would observe how often glitter has been associated not just with queerness and/or sexuality but also with contamination or infection. We've already heard Demetri Martin's comic comparison of glitter to herpes. Ponder also this line from A.E. Stallings' 2018 sonnet, "Glitter": "It's catching, like the chicken pox, or lice"[43]—afflictions, of course, primarily linked to children.

Remein reminds us of the role of race in these associations, concluding that "the command not to decorate . . . encodes [a] blend of . . . racism, misogyny, and homophobia." He recounts, for example, Modernist (and fascist and anti-Semite) writer Ezra Pound's famous "exhortations to poets to 'use absolutely no word that does not contribute to the presentation,'" as well as Modernist critic and designer (and sexual abuser) Adolf Loos' claim that "'What is natural to the

Papuan [a generic term referencing an Indigenous person from New Guinea] and the child is a symptom of degeneracy in the modern adult.'" As Loos reasoned—and in italics, so you know he was serious—*"'the evolution of culture is synonymous with the removal of ornament from utilitarian objects.'"*[44] In other words, respectable (read: white) culture is defined by simplicity and restraint rather than decoration.

To connect all the dots, then: the environmentalist bias against glitter, and against decorative and supposedly frivolous objects more generally, could be said to encode or at least serve homophobic, transphobic, misogynist, "effeminophobic," racist, nationalist, xenophobic, fascist, and classist values.[45] At best, it is unsympathetic to how important glitter has been, materially as well as symbolically, to marginalized communities.

Even if you're not fully convinced by those points, you might be compelled to ask what the upshot of the glitter backlash might be. If we ban glitter today, what happens tomorrow? Do we start going about in recycled burlap sacks, since fashion is also decorative and "unnecessary"? If we want to be environmentalists, can we do *anything* unnecessary, frivolous, or fun—such as eating desserts or drinking cocktails? (I hate to be a killjoy myself, but it turns out that those tasty treats create a bunch of unnecessary waste.[46]) And while we're at it, should we all give up our laptops, tablets, and cell phones—since their planned obsolescence is incredibly wasteful, not to mention the fact that most are constructed with unethical labor practices? Who will be first to volunteer?

While I am clearly quite skeptical of what I've dubbed the Great Glitter Backlash, its proponents and I agree wholeheartedly on at least one point: glitter *does* things. It is not an inert, passive object, but rather something that makes impacts and has consequences, often unpredictable and far-reaching ones.

In fact, this is a good moment to point out that "glitter" was a verb long before it was a noun. It emerged around the early 1400s, according to the *Oxford English Dictionary*, denoting, "[t]o shine with a brilliant but broken and tremulous light; to emit bright fitful flashes of light; to gleam, sparkle." The noun form of the word dates to 1602 and refers to "sparkling light; brightness, brilliance, lustre, splendour." Both forms come from the Germanic root *glīt*, which indicated shine. Only in the last century has "glitter" referred to the specific craft and/or cosmetic product. This is all to say that "glitter" has long referred to *action*. And throughout this book we will see that, even when we take "glitter" as a noun, it still retains that sense of action: dynamism, movement, activity.

Of course, it would be difficult to claim that the primary function of glitter—the noun as we now know it—is anything other than decorative. Many people go days, if not longer, without actively engaging with it. It's not something one needs to live. And yet it remains ubiquitous. As I have suggested above, it has been the source of major controversy and a popular commodity in many forms, appearing in and on everything from nail polish to toys to crafts to greeting cards to cupcakes to—wait for it—boats and wallpaper.[47] As

I will go on to show in the following chapters, it has served as a political tool and the inspiration for multi-million-dollar entertainment projects. It crosses cultural boundaries—and this book will as well, with stops in sites ranging from Brazil to Mexico to Palestine to Scotland—and crops up across multiple languages. (Particularly beautiful equivalents, to my ears, include "vezulliam" [Albanian], "ōlinolino" [Hawai'ian], "kirakira" [Japanese], and "purpurina" [Peninsular Spanish].)

With such a wide scope, I can't pretend to offer a comprehensive history of glitter. I also admit that my discussions are biased toward the contemporary period—but perhaps that's understandable, considering scholar Mary Celeste Kearney's claim that "the amount of sparkle in US culture has multiplied exponentially since the start of the new millennium, making our world twinkle and shine as if it is bedazzled with pixie dust"[48]—"sparkle" being her term not just for glitter but for a broad array of products and visuals with shiny, feminine appeal.

And nor do I wish to argue for the historical importance of glitter itself—the way one could with the lightbulb, the telephone, or the shipping container.[49] Instead, this book will try to give you a sense of glitter as a cultural substance that demonstrates the shifting intersection of multiple concerns—including gender, sexuality, race, class, environment, pollution, science, consumerism, entertainment, and emotions. Ultimately, I will propose that glitter is a unique site at which we might begin to creatively confront the reality that some scholars have labeled the "Plasticene": following the Holocene, a geological era of environmental crisis marked by the omnipresence of plastic. This book therefore seeks to highlight the potency of an object that stands at the margins of our daily lives.

Glitter Bar: A Makeover Takeover!

On the evening of June 26, 2021, several enthusiastic people congregated through the Internet ether for "Glitter Bar: A Makeover Takeover!" co-hosted by yours truly and drag queen Mystika Glamoor. Those who signed up for the event received two 1-gram biodegradable bags of ecoglitter in the mail from us, via UK-based brand EcoStardust. This event was part of the 2021 Edinburgh Science Festival, which typically draws 175,000 people in person, but which was reconceived for Zoom and other outlets due to the pandemic. What follows is a partial transcript of the event.

Nicole: We're at 7:30 on the dot. Are people on time to drag events? Is it homophobic to begin exactly on the dot?

Mystika: The whole thing about a drag show is that the poster says, "starting at 9" and you turn up and it starts at approximately 11:33. That's just standard.

Nicole: Hello everyone, and welcome to our "Glitter Bar COLON A Makeover Takeover!" event. We want to thank the Edinburgh Science Festival for having us. I'm shocked that they said yes! But here we are. My name is Nicole Seymour but tonight I have changed my Zoom name to Dr. Seymour Sparkles. That is the energy that I'm bringing to this Zoom-box tonight.

Mystika: Well, good evening fellow cisgender heterosexuals—and, of course, members of the BLT community, if you're here. My name is Mystika Glamoor. I call myself the "surrealist socialist socialite." I also call myself the "high priestess of Edinburgh drag" because I read tarot cards and also sometimes get drunk and just shout advice at people. My alter ego Oskar is also the co-owner of Kafe Kweer, a café for the local queer community.

Nicole: This event has been designed to be participatory and interactive, so we really encourage you to turn your cameras on so we can see your gorgeous visages. If you need a moment to adjust your wig, that's fine, but when you're ready, click on that camera icon and show us what you got!

Our agenda: we'll be having a glitter demo from Mystika while I tell you about the science and history of glitter, and then Mystika is going to lead all of us in making ourselves over with the glitter you received. And then finally we should have some time at the end for chitchat.

So, here's the bad news: glitter has historically been made of microplastics. Boo!! According to scientist Dannielle Senga Green and co-authors, glitter "is a unique type of microplastic, typically consisting of three layers; a plastic core usually made of a type of stretched polyester PET film known as BoPET (biaxially-oriented polyethylene terephthalate), often coated with aluminium to create a reflective appearance and topped with another thin plastic layer, e.g. styrene acrylate."[1]

But does anyone know where most microplastics in the ocean are coming from? Any guesses?

Mystika: Wigs!

Nicole: Wigs, absolutely. It's 99.9% wigs. It's a disaster. No, actually, it's things like fleece jackets. If you have a North Face jacket, Jack Wolfskin, Patagonia—I mean, no one in this crowd is wearing that kind of crunchy stuff, but—every time you wash one of those things, since they're synthetic fibers, the fibers come off and head out to the ocean. Also tires.

So glitter is not a major source of microplastics. But at some point a couple years ago people realized we should have low- and no-plastic alternatives, so they started inventing brands like this one we have today, EcoStardust. These glitters are made with cellulose from eucalyptus as their core instead of plastic. What we have is the "Pure" range, which is plastic-free, aluminum-free as well, and also vegetarian. Why do I mention that? A lot of cosmetics are not vegetarian because they contain ground-up cochineal insects for carmine, which is a red pigment.

So, no insects were harmed in the making of this product, but we do have, according to their Web site, "Rayon (Cellulose Regenerated), Glycerin (Plant Derived), Aqua, Urea, Shellac, [+/- Mica, Synthetic

Fluorphlogopite, Titanium Dioxide (CI: 77891), Iron Oxide (CI: 77489), Ferric Ammonium Ferrocyanide (CI: 77510), Tin Oxide (CI: 77861)."[2] This line is independently certified as biodegradable, including in freshwater, so in 4-5 weeks it will degrade in the natural environment. The founder of this company also says it's 40% softer than regular glitter because, again, it doesn't have the plastic or the aluminum, so you're not going to get that scratchiness.[3]

If you're allergic to any of those ingredients, don't put this glitter on your face! Don't have a terrible medical reaction. We don't have any money, so you can't sue us. But if you do have some kind of reaction, wash it off with warm water and never speak of this again!

How's it going over there, Mystika?

Mystika: It has been a while since I did a glitter beard. Especially as someone who doesn't have a beard, it's been a struggle pushing out every little hair for this night. But yeah, I got there! I've got this lovely rich, purple glitter in there and you can see it trembling in the light. Ah! Fluttering.

Nicole: So we're doing it: group makeover time! We are all in Mystika's hands, for better or worse.

Mystika: Definitely for the worse. So, I'm thinking what we're going to do with all the glitter is a little bit on the cheeks, a little bit on the brow bone because it gives you that extra pop, then the ultimate pro tip of drag: just on the tip of the nose. Not the tip at the end of your nose, but just above it. You want it to still be on the line of your nose. And do remember to take a selfie before—this is the whole transformational process of drag!

The most important thing about drag performance, or just existing as a human being, is delusion—just convince yourself that you are the most beautiful creature in the world. You say, "Oh my god it's so good to see youuu!!!" That's you talking to yourself in the mirror. And that's drag, essentially.

I've got this little brush, but you can use your fingers if you want to.

Nicole: That's why God gave us fingers, to put on our glitter.

I'm curious what colors of glitter you all received. These have fabulous names—I got "Flame" and "Mirrorball."

Mystika: The one I'm using is a name which just describes me perfectly: "Ultra Chunky Sherbet."

Highlighting and glitter and all this stuff adds so much dimension, so when you move there's this extra shimmering layer.

Nicole: Someone in the chat says they got the color "Rainbow Fish." [Other participants reported receiving "Aphrodite," "Cascade," "Jellyfish," and "Sunshine."] That reminds me of the parrotfish, which is a transsexual fish. It's true; there are transsexual fish!

Mystika: There's so many variances of how to be, what your gender is, in nature, and then people are like, "There are only two genders!" And it's like, "I am proof that that is a lie." One of my favorite lines to open shows with was, "Gender is dead and I'm the Grim Reaper."

Nicole: By the way, I'm so touched by watching people apply glitter to other people. It's so sweet!

Mystika: One thing I've learned is, if you smile, you have these nice little "apples," and that's a really nice spot to put a bit of glitter as well; just adds even more dimension. Just a nice padded round circle on the pillows of the cheek, let's call them that.

Also, I see what you mean about this glitter being really soft. I've used glitter that is basically just broken glass scraping across my face.

Are we feeling the delusion starting to kick in?

Nicole: I just spilled the glitter all over my keyboard, by the way. Glitter does not respect boundaries, that's what I've learned. I have to turn my glitter book manuscript in in a week and so maybe my computer is just going to finish it for me!

Mystika: This is the manuscript now.

Glitter will haunt you till the rest of your days. I've burnt down houses, I've fled the country, and that glitter's still there. Just one tiny little micrograin in my suitcase, taunting me, just looking up and going, "haha, remember me??"

Looking good—very nice darlings, very nice. It does pop more when you have it on certain spots of the face rather than just everywhere. What I'm going to do now is the top of the brows. If you raise your brows you should be able to see a little line there—just fill that in a wee bit.

Nicole: This same brand has a "Bio-Glitter Beauty Balm" that I'm using as an application glue, which is not petroleum-based (because petroleum is oil and that's evil, yada yada).

Don't forget your "After" selfie if you're wrapping up. So, because I'm an English professor and a big dork, I want to hear what adjectives you all are feeling. I'm feeling "shimmery" . . . "otherworldly" . . . so drop some adjectives in the chat!

[Adjectives offered included "Mermaidy," "Mystical and a bit sunburnt," "Effervescent," "Glistering," and "Like a British sparkling wine." We then "spotlit" our participants, who gamely posed for us and angled their faces toward the light to best show off their sparkles.]

Mystika: This is what I love about glitter. It's a moving picture, it has to be.

Nicole: These are professional models here. We've been infiltrated.

2 "FEEL THE RAINBOW!"

GLITTER AS TACTIC

GLITTER is wheat paste, graffiti, and unlawful use of space. GLITTER is without permit.

—T.L. COWAN, "GLITTERfesto: An Open Call in Trinity Formation for a Revolutionary Movement of Activist Performance Based on the Premise That Social Justice Is Fabulous"

A month before the 2020 Presidential election in the United States, my old friend Derek Mong, a poet and translator living in small-town Crawfordsville, Indiana, disclosed on Facebook, "Every year we endure the cowardly harassment of our neighbors: election signs torn down, gay pride flags stolen, stuff thrown in the yard. It happened again last night." One of his friends responded by advising him to put

Vaseline on the edges of his signs and cover them with glitter, explaining in a post, "At least you will have some revenge, especially if they put the sign in their car. Glitter will be there forever." Five days later, after strategizing with his son Whitman, Derek updated us: "Now on the lookout for a glam-glittered and fully vaselined Crawfordsvillian. That'll be our Biden-Harris sign thief."

Were Derek to seriously pursue this *Scooby-Doo*-esque case, he would be interested to know that there is extensive legal precedent for glitter as forensic evidence, including in at least three US homicide cases.[1] Because of the many unique factors of a given batch of this substance—color, shape, thickness, size—retired criminalist Bob Blackledge enthuses that it "might even surpass carpet fibers as being the most nearly perfect contact trace!"[2] (The phrase "contract trace" may remind some readers of anti-Covid-19 protocols—furthering the associations between glitter and disease that I have discussed.)

But what strikes me most about this particular set of hijinks is how glitter functions not just as a tool of revenge but also as a political tactic. This is to say that Derek and Whitman's specific choice of glitter was not incidental, but rather one calculated against the likes of someone who would steal gay pride flags or leftist campaign signs. Such functioning obviously contrasts the common idea of glitter as frivolous, useless, or merely decorative. Or, perhaps more accurately, as I will show, glitter's *perceived* uselessness and frivolity is a large part of what makes it potentially *effective* as political tactic. This chapter will focus primarily on the role of glitter in recent feminist demonstrations in Mexico, with detours to other sites at which glitter has been used by activists over the past decade, including in LGBTQ+ actions against homophobic politicians in the US and anti-fascist counterdemonstrations in Scotland.

The spread of glittery tactics across such different sites mirrors how glitter . . . well, spreads across different sites: "[o]ne of its properties is its tendency to disperse, spread and scatter."[3] More pointedly, it exemplifies a "modular tactic": as activist and philosopher L.M. Bogad elaborates, "[g]roups all over the world can pull common tactics from their action toolkits, and perform [them] globally in solidarity and simultaneity."[4] While responding to the unique sociopolitical circumstances in question, all of these examples play off of audiences' love-it-or-hate-it relationships with glitter, while also exploiting its unique physical properties and cultural associations.

"The Glitter Will Not Fade"

As Mexican writer Jorge Volpi explains, in the four years leading up to an unprecedented series of protests starting in August 2019,

femicides [in Mexico] increased by 150 percent, while almost all rapes and cases of harassment or trafficking [have gone] unpunished. Indignation and anger should be shared by all citizens, but it has been women, and particularly those under 25, who have finally dared to [mount] the only one visible resistance to an order that not only allows but encourages violence . . . against women and vulnerable groups, such as girls and the LGTB + community.[5]

This movement to which Volpi refers quickly became known as *la Revolución Diamantina* or "the Glitter Revolution"—so-called because a protestor doused the security minister of Mexico City, Jesús Orta Martínez, in pink glitter at the initial protest on August 12, 2019. This tactic was picked up in subsequent actions over the next several weeks, which spread to 16 Mexican states. Artist Rubén Ortiz Torres commemorated this movement in his 2020 work *Glitter Protest on the Door—Protesta brillantina en puerta*, wherein a pink sparkly splotch covers the insignia of a police car door—the latter a symbol of the patriarchal state violence being opposed.

The aforementioned "glitterbombings" exploit the unique qualities of this substance, including stickiness, persistence, dispersibility, visibility, and irritation. Those things just so happen to also be political goals. Consider, for example, stickiness and persistence. One of the Mexican protestors' slogans was, "The women you murdered will not die"—the obvious implication being that the protests would ensure the persistence of their memory. Similarly, the feminist

FIGURE 1 *Glitter Protest on the Door—Prctesta brillantina en puerta*, 2020. Urethane, candy paint, flake and holographic flake on shot decommissioned Tijuana Police car door. 56 x 31 x 13 in—142.2 x 78.7 x 33 cm. Courtesy of artist Rubén Ortiz Torres.

collective Luchadoras promises in a related section of their Web site, *La diamantina no se borrará*, or, "The glitter will not fade."[6] Glitter's dispersibility, due to its lightness and relatively small size, also means that it exceeds control in multiple ways. It refuses to be contained, spreading across multiple sites just as protestors flood through streets, take over freeways, swarm and occupy buildings. Glitter also symbolizes political activism itself, insofar as individual acts make little difference compared to the power, and the joys, of *collective* action and resistance. No one bit of glitter is glitter; no one bit of glitter glitters. And this is true on the most basic of etymological levels: as a collective noun, "glitter" has multiplicity built into it.

I'm suggesting that glitter can be read as a metaphor or inspiration for political goals. But it can also literally or materially enact those goals. For example, protestors make themselves extra-visible as feminine and/or queer through the use of glitter. As scholar Vanbasten Noronha de Araújo explains, glitter gives "visibility to neglected populations, depicting their existence as powerful." To wear glitter, then, is to refuse to "sh[y] away from being seen, recognized," or from expressing yourself.[7] Let's take the example of Glitter+Ash, a movement organized for Ash Wednesday, the day when Christians receive a cross marking on their foreheads to signal the beginning of Lent. The US LGBTQ+ Christian organization Parity introduced the idea of mixing glitter in with the ash used for marking; on their Web site, below the declaration, "WE WILL BE SEEN," they state, "Glitter Ashes lets the world know that we are progressive, queer-positive Christians."[8] Similarly, the use of glitter in celebrations such as Carnival and Mardi Gras publicly mark those who attend.

But of course, not all LGBTQ+ individuals perceive glitter, or visibility, in the same way. A "queer anarchist" group in the US vandalized the building of the Human Rights Campaign in 2009 and 2011 with pink paint and glitter, self-reporting that they were opposed to the organization's "assimilationist" goals such as marriage rights and inclusion in the military.[9] That is, *some* LGBTQ+ folks want to fit in rather than stand out; glitter assists one in doing the latter, while simultaneously critiquing the former. As that anonymous blogger referenced in the previous chapter puts it, "Glitter is inescapable. It's never stealth, and it has no passing privilege."[10]

In addition to securing their own visibility, glitter protestors ensure that their targets cannot easily forget their demands, thanks to their chosen material's clinginess and persistence—which is caused in the first place, experts theorize, by forces such as static electricity and surface tension.[11] As US activist Nick Espinosa stated of his decision to glitterbomb homophobic politician Newt Gingrich in Minneapolis in 2011—the glitterbombing felt around the world, which spark(l)ed many more—"'I . . . knew that it would stick with him'" and that for "'days to come he'd be remembering what I said as he pulled the glitter sparkles from his hair.'"[12] And what Espinosa had said was, "Feel the rainbow, Newt! Stop the hate! Stop anti-gay politics!"

Glittery Emotions

La Revolución Diamantina was for the most part an emotionally intense affair—full of righteous rage. But the appearance of glitterbombing, along with other instances in the US and elsewhere, exemplifies what Amory Starr has called "tactical frivolity"—in which activists reflect "back in the form of the protest the *absurdity* of the policies and institutions in power."[13] Examples range from gay activist Tom Higgins serving anti-gay campaigner Anita Bryant a pie in the face during a 1977 press conference; to Texas' 1993 "Moon the Klan" event, when 5,000 Austinites greeted a busload of white supremacists with their exposed bare butts; to a group of clowns at the University of California, Davis in 2011 who reenacted with silly string an incident in which a police officer viciously pepper-sprayed Occupy movement protestors. In these examples, playfulness doesn't minimize hatred and violence, but it does show them to be ridiculous—not to mention a lot less fun than their alternatives. Further, the frivolity of these performances can (at least figuratively) disarm and disorient the opponent, who might have come expecting a more militant response.[14]

Indeed, we could say that the gap between the emotions or sensibilities of such protestors and those of their opponents is precisely where the protestors' critique becomes most clear. We see this in Harry Josephine Giles' description of a 2018 event in Scotland dubbed "Glitter against Fascism":

Forty-odd queers and allies gathered at the foot of Leith Walk, covered in sequins and sparkles and glitter, holding signs that said things like . . . "Migrants Welcome — Fascists Out," chanting "No borders! No nations! End deportation!" And they laughed at a group of twenty-odd miserable-looking fascists from the Scottish Defense League, National Front and National Action, they chanted far more loudly and jubilantly whenever the fascists chanted, they sang "So long, farewell, auf wiedersehn [*sic*], goodbye!" [lyrics from my favorite movie, the 1965 musical *The Sound of Music*, which happens to feature an anti-Nazi plot] when the fascists went home early.[15]

In Giles' account, fascism brings misery while anti-fascism brings jubilance—aided and abetted in large part by glitter. And of course, fittingly for a pro-migrant demonstration, glitter's dispersibility means it respects no borders.

Beyond ideological aims, tactical frivolity has practical benefits. Bogad claims that, to "recruit new members and grow the movement," protest actions "should be attractive or charismatic. Even if the issue is deadly serious . . . the time spent and the physical movement through space [should] inspire desire and defiant joy."[16] And in fact, glitterbombing participants reported to sociologist Anya Galli that they felt more at ease participating in events such as protests of gay "conversion" clinics because the "joyousness of glitter offset the gravity of the issues at hand." Interestingly, glitter bombers report their own experiences of conversion. One woman had never considered herself politically active before meeting Espinosa, the groundbreaking Minneapolis glitterbomber; she now jokes that he "converted" her with glitter.[17] This comment playfully riffs on homophobic notions of "gay recruitment" as well as queer contagion, discussed below.

To be clear, reveling in this joy and playfulness does not mean that glittery protestors downplay the aforementioned "gravity of the issues"—or of the dangers of protest, which have recently been brought to the fore in the United States through the murders of anti-racist activists such as Heather Heyer. Perhaps another set of lines from T.L. Cowan's "GLITTERfesto" captures the complicated situation best: "GLITTER strategically pretends like everything is okay. This is a survival strategy. GLITTER knows that everything is not okay."

Glitter's Logistics

We know now how glitter works ideologically and emotionally as a political tool. But how does it work logistically—that is, on the ground? I turn here to queer Hungarian artist and "troublemaker" Artúr van Balen, known for designing and displaying inflatables in protest actions. He explains that acts of tactical frivolity do at least two important things: "providing an iconic meme for the media (see *PRINCIPLE: Do the media's work for them*)" and "forcing authorities into a decision dilemma (see *PRINCIPLE: Put your target in a decision dilemma*)"—meaning not only that they must make a decision based on your actions, but that all their available options play to *your* advantage.[18] Since many readers already know that glitterbombing has proven quite iconic—if you've been on the Internet in the past ten years, you've probably seen some related meme or other—I'll spend my time here applying the second concept, the "decision dilemma," to glitterbombing. I think it goes something like this:

Given glitter's association with queer people and women, if the male target—and glitterbombees have almost always been male, and cisgender, as far as I can tell—ignores the glitter, he allows himself to be marked with this sparkly substance and thus risks looking feminized or queered—and therefore too much like the bomber, from whom he presumably wishes to distance himself. "[E]ven unintentionally," Cowan remarks, glitter "is a public declaration of affinity."[19] The target will also likely look ridiculous and immature if he ignores the glitter—rather than full of gravitas, which most male politicians, except for perhaps Donald Trump, strive for. On the other hand, if he reacts with disgust or phobia, such as by furiously attempting to brush the glitter away, he thereby proves the bomber's implicit charges that he is misogynist, homophobic, or, in the case of columnist Dan Savage (who was glitterbombed by trans activists), transphobic and homonormative. And given the impossibility of fully cleaning up glitter, the target will also look inept and powerless as he tries to do so.

If police or security drag the glitterbomber away (as happened with the person who glitterbombed US politician Rick Santorum) or if the target presses charges later (as US politician Mitt Romney did after being glitterbombed), the target may appear hysterical or thin-skinned—and therefore, again, feminized or queered. But again, if he does nothing, he forfeits the opportunity to condemn his opponents. Here, glitter's status as supposedly frivolous and useless becomes important yet again. What grown man could possibly be afraid of glitter?

As we saw earlier in this book, environmentalists have some concerns, as do glitterbombing targets such as Santorum and Romney—a rare, but certainly not unheard of, instance of environmentalists and conservatives standing in alignment. They're not entirely off-base, as there have been reports of people experiencing glitter-related injuries—though such incidents are isolated and rare, and none, to my knowledge, occurred due to glitterbombings. (I discuss these injuries in the next chapter.) But it's probably worth recalling glitter's unique and variable material qualities. When Espinosa chose glitter for his action against Gingrich, "he did so in part because glitter was lightweight" and "'wouldn't be construed as violen[t].'" Other glitterbombers "were also careful to choose glitter that was large enough that it could not be inhaled or get into targets' eyes or airways."[20] So here we start to see the many sets of paradoxes around glitter: Is it useless, or is it a tool? Is it harmless, or is it dangerous?

The competing answers to those questions have very real implications, especially when we consider, for example, the overcriminalization of protest that has led to skewed definitions of violence. And indeed, two anti-pipeline protestors were recently charged with a "terrorism hoax" stemming from the glitter that fell off the banner they unfurled at an energy company's headquarters.[21] Such treatment lends a grim gloss to the "bombing" part of "glitterbombing," an otherwise playful concept. Let us consider the words of activist Sandra Aguilar-Gomez, who was frustrated that the Mexican media harped on the defacement of the Angel of Peace monument in Mexico City in those *Revolución Diamantina* protests: "'They can't see the pain in the faces of the mothers and sisters of murdered women, and the raped women, and the harassed women . . . But they are very, very, very empathetic with this lady made of stone.'"[22] Something similar is happening when we harp on the relatively negligible environmental effects of glitter, rather than contextualizing them within larger pictures of feminist, queer, anti-racist, and other activisms.

Toward that end, we should turn here to sociologist Rebecca Coleman, who has linked the idea of the fabulousness of glitter with the concept of fabulation in order to think of glitterbombing as an example of prefigurative politics. As she explains, glitterbombing "creates the world it wants to see in the present. The sparkly showers dramatize queer collectivity and spread joy."[23] To claim that glitterbombing *instead*, or *also*, spreads pollution would not be entirely wrong.

But it would be to fundamentally misread the spirit of the action. It would also be to forget the beautiful connection that performance artist and scholar Kareem Khubchandani identified for me: that between the movement of glitter and the notion of social/political movements. Glitter potentially shifts politics as it spreads through space.

Now is probably a good time to mention that instructions for eco-friendly homemade glitter, namely that made from sugar, circulated on social media networks during the *Revolución Diamantina* protests. Similarly, groups such as the Philadelphia-based cabaret troupe The Bearded Ladies and the Washington, D.C.-based activist collective WERK for Peace have pointedly used biodegradable glitter in their actions.[24] The former announced their switch to biodegradable glitter on Facebook, later joking about show tickets, "Price is now $8 for glitter inflation."[25] In many cases, then, glitterbombers demonstrate care for the environment as well as care for their opponents.

Tensions and Contested Meanings

If glitter is both coded as queer and understood as dispersible and thus in some sense "contagious"—meaning, it transfers from one body to another—it potentially activates homophobic associations between queerness and toxicity/disease. Various right-wing conspiracy theorists have picked up on these associations in recent years. White supremacist Alex Jones, for instance, has infamously insisted that the US water supply is poisoned with chemicals that are "'making the friggin' frogs gay.'"[26] Meanwhile, as I have already shown, glitter has served as a metaphor for various diseases. In fact, I would suggest that glitter's close association with queerness is precisely what allows it to get taken up in fantasies of disease.

Some glitterbombers actually embrace this notion of contagion, just as I've suggested they embrace "conversion"— which exemplifies how the cultural meanings of glitter are always being contested and negotiated. Berlin-based entrepreneur Jeanne Low told me in an interview that she started her biodegradable glitter company, Projekt Glitter, in 2016, at a point when she was frequently attending festivals and

> always taking glitter with me to share with people. When you share this very simple product with people, they're instantly transformed. They allow you into a very intimate space. And then they're just so happy. I love taking glitter with me to share, as a gift. It's a very easy way to become best friends with everybody.[27]

Low reframes the contagiousness of glitter and its related emotions as positive; as relational and intimate.

One could argue that glittery protestors run the potential risk of confirming glitter/femininity/queerness as negative things by weaponizing them. Further, one might find their moves of forced feminization or forced queerness—even if temporary—to be unethical. Amber Aumiller, a University of Utah student who spoke to me after a talk, recalled living in a glitter-obsessed communal house that eventually had to have a reckoning after party guests complained of coming home bedazzled—echoing conversations across college campuses about sexual consent. As someone once quipped on Twitter, "Glitter, like so many things, requires enthusiastic, continuous CONSENT."[28]

And indeed, some non-LGBTQ+ pranksters have exploited the vexing persistence of this substance toward apolitical and even discriminatory ends. Australian entrepreneur Matthew Carpenter, for example, launched www.shipyourenemies glitter.com in 2015—but put the site up for sale almost immediately because of overwhelming demand. "'Please stop buying this horrible glitter product—I'm sick of dealing with it,'" Carpenter warned potential customers.[29] We might also recall the 2018 case in which the desk of a gay student officer at University College London was glitterbombed, an apparently homophobic act that left the student feeling unsafe.[30] As Amber's fellow student Gardiner Allen said to me, many people perceive glitter as a form of punishment.

But perhaps it's worth differentiating between those who love glitter and weaponize it, and those who hate glitter and weaponize it (and, in Carpenter's case, monetize it). Sometimes, then, it's not the material of glitter that matters per se, but rather the intentions or feelings behind it. Or, to put a finer point on it, whether or not you perceive glitter as a weapon is a reflection of your values. Further, if we recall the ideas of glitter as intimacy and glitter as relational—it moves between and across people, it connects individuals, it exists to be noticed by others, etc.—we might instead see an act such as glitterbombing as an invitation, even a kind of mock baptism. I have to think here of my favorite glitterbombing story: how a group of activists boarded the "Sky Ride" attraction at the 2011 Minnesota State Fair and deluged an anti-same-sex marriage group's booth from above. "Join us!!" glitter shouts, as it rains on its opponents or catches their eye.

Glitter, Cheap and Tacky

Plastic glitter is cheap, economically speaking, as is homemade glitter. This cheapness constitutes another of glitter's fundamental properties/politics. For one thing, cheapness matters specifically for glitterbombing; the act is seen as accessible to those who adopt it because glitter is cheap and easy to obtain—not to mention that it is "easy to conceal," and that glitterbombing actions are "easy to film and share on social media." Further, glitter's cheap and easy character has enabled the "tactical diffusion" of glitterbombing, as "a tactic's flexibility and ability to be easily emulated will have a positive influence on its adoption."[31]

The economics of glitter is political in other senses as well. Consider how the (plastic) glitter backlash I described earlier has extended to Carnival, which has its roots in the communities of enslaved African people in Brazil.[32] While some entrepreneurs have developed low- or no-plastic glitters for Carnival, many participants report that they're too expensive. Expressing her skepticism about the environmental impact of glitter, celebrant Angelica Nobrega told a reporter, "'It is just one more thing to make the lives of Brazilians more difficult . . . I think they are making it up.'"[33] While Nobrega may be *factually* incorrect, I want us to take her sentiments seriously; some perceive the glitter backlash as classist, not just homophobic. Plastic or homemade glitter may be cheap, but can everyone afford to "go green"?

More broadly, glitter and other shiny things often serve as accessible shortcuts for the poor, or as means to reverse power hierarchies. Consider, for example, how England's Queen Elizabeth I legislated in 1565 against the lower classes wearing jewels, metallic threads, and other items she favored, because doing so would supposedly cause "disorder and confusion."[34] In this way, Ph.D. student Molly Mapstone told me she thinks of glitter as "economically subversive": "formally, and materially, it is reflective and iridescent like other more expensive materials (gold, diamond, silver). It possesses the same effects without the cost."

Of course, if glittery, shiny things have become correlated with the poor rather than the elite in contemporary times, they can become further stigmatized. Some of you may have been waiting for me to quote the famous line, "All that glitters is not gold"—an aphorism adapted from Shakespeare's 1598 play *The Merchant of Venice* to suggest "the fraudulence of glittering things."[35] That is, while the public once met glittering things with admiration or aspiration, they might now meet them with suspicion and disdain. And if one is more specifically thinking of glitter, and glitter as plastic, then a similar perception holds: "at some point [in the postwar era], plastics stopped seeming cool and new and began seeming false and tacky."[36]

This brings me to a new task: trying to think through the relationship between the term "tacky" as in sticky, clingy, or adhesive—which we know glitter is—and the term "tacky" as in cheap, trashy, and/or loud—which glitter also, arguably, is. There is no clear etymological link between the two terms, according to the *Oxford English Dictionary*, but in this case I think they come together. Glitter sticks or adheres to bodies, and those bodies, especially if they are raced or classed in particular ways, may then get stigmatized as cheap or trashy, including in the environmentalist sense.

Think of the anxieties of Mariah Carey's backup singers and best friends in the film *Glitter* (2001), a Black woman and a Latina woman respectively, as they prepare to dress up in shiny clothes for a big event:

"You look like a disco ball."
"It goes with the hoops."
"It's too much."

In her work on Black and Latina "aesthetic excess," gender studies scholar Jillian Hernandez explains these internalized standards: "[r]acialized and hypersexual femininity in particular has served as a denigrated prism through which the superiority of authentic, truthful, and natural/simple (white) styles have been asserted."[37] Interest in the glittery, shiny, and colorful, in other words, may mark one as backwards or inferior by dominant Euro-western standards. We're right back with those Modernist European tastemakers we met last chapter. Here's another one for your list: the French-Swiss architect and designer (and Nazi sympathizer) Le Corbusier, who "abhorred glitter, posing aesthetic purity against the fashionable patterns beloved" by groups such as "the working classes, women, natives—those who would be distracted by shiny stuff."[38]

But asserting interest in "shiny stuff" nonetheless may challenge, or at least defy, those standards. We might consider here art historian Krista Thompson's work on how urban African diasporic communities "disrupt notions of value by privileging not things but their visual effects."[39] While Thompson is referring to practices such as wearing "bling," and not glitter specifically, I think the same point holds. While glitter may be tacky in both of the ways I just described—clingy and trashy—the worth of the material itself is less important to users than its visual, affective, symbolic, and other effects.[40] Those effects are political in and of themselves, and also play important roles in political actions, as we have seen.

Some might wonder if glitterbombing, in all its frivolity and playfulness, actually undermines sustained political commitment. Many glitterbombers report that they have no ties to existing organizations and little history of prior activism. Further, glitterbombing largely lost popularity in the US as a political tactic within about a year of Espinosa's action against Gingrich. It appeared in not one but two episodes of the popular US television program *Glee* in late 2011 and early 2015, giving many the sense that the tactic had become mainstream and defanged. As Bogad notes, "[s]urprise is important at a tactical level . . . Surprise activates us . . . it is a moment of openness and freshness, in which new perspectives, response, and reflections are possible"— whereas, in contrast, "[c]liché dulls the senses and bores the mind."[41] By 2015, if not much earlier, glitterbombing had become cliché to many.[42]

But this is precisely why its reappearance in Scotland in 2018 and Mexico in 2019 is so interesting. Glitter can do new work in different contexts—just as, as I show later in this book, its constitution has changed over time, from minerals to plastic to cellulose. Glitter is a matter of innovation and responsiveness, and we don't know where it will explode next.

Poetry Reading: CAConrad

If there were a Poet Laureate of Glitter (and why isn't there??), CAConrad would be the inaugural one. The Lambda Literary Award-winning queer trans writer is known for their "Soma(tic) Poetry Rituals": they design exercises that demand their close attention—such as "blowing bubbles, inspecting parking-lot trees,"[1] and "riding escalators and showing photographs of [themself] to strangers [and] asking, 'Excuse me, have you seen this person?'"[2]—then take extensive notes on the experience, and finally transform those notes into poems.

Across their 9 books of poetry and essays, Conrad engages with glitter in ways that range from the profound to the wacky. "Glitter in My Wounds" (2018), for example, offers us this meditation:

. . . glitter on a queer is not to dazzle but to
unsettle the foundations of this murderous culture[3]

Meanwhile, a lyric essay titled, "The Queer Voice: Reparative Poetry Rituals & Glitter Perversions" (2015), imagines a "new glitter invention" that will turn semen into "glitter jizz!" Conrad cheerily acknowledges that "[o]f course there will be side-effects, children born with lime green complexions or coughing tinsel-coated phlegm, but everyone has to sacrifice something for the fun and gleaming new world!"

Throughout their work, glitter appears as a simultaneously practical and fanciful device, one with which to respond to the hateful slings and arrows of life while conjuring a better one. In this, Conrad resembles a literary version of the glitterbombers we just met. In "The Queer Voice," for example, Conrad reports that, when they began receiving homophobic emails from Elvis fans after writing a book on The King, they "replied with a photo of my middle finger, the nail encrusted in bright violet glitter. For the photo I aimed every light in the house on that nail until it was the most glamorous FUCK YOU I have ever seen in my life! I was almost in tears looking at it so blindingly purple and magnificent."[4] These lines summarize some of the ideas of the last chapter—such as glitter as the substance of celebration *and* revenge—and preview those we will encounter in the next chapter—such as glitter as visually spellbinding yet "blinding."

As we can see above, Conrad uses various stylistic techniques to engage with glitter, including vivid imagery, internal slant rhymes ("dazzle"/"unsettle"), and assonance ("bright violet"). To think a little further through the poetics of glitter, I will present a brief close reading of another one of Conrad's glitter-themed poems before turning to their work on the kindred substance of bubbles.

In "OBLIVIOUS IMPERIALISM IS THE WORST KIND," Conrad's speaker recounts that

someone
recently said
"HEY your nails

are beautiful but
the rest of your
outfit is just okay"

The poem continues with an apparent rejoinder from the speaker:

glamour is my
great love but is
too expensive and
too much work
my beautiful
glittered nails are
my HOMAGE to GLAMOUR[5]

More than conveying major concepts about glitter—including that it is both cheap and associated with extravagance—this poem captures aspects of glitter on a formal level. For one thing, we could say that the lack of end punctuation, also found in "Glitter in My Wounds," echoes glitter's insidious messiness; how it spreads and exceeds containment. For another, the all-caps words in "OBLIVIOUS IMPERIALISM" echo how glitter STANDS OUT from the mundane, the dreary lower-case of everyday life. Glitter hails passersby such as the unknown "someone," who in turn hails the speaker (to pun on the similarly sparkly, particulate, aggregate, and atmospheric—though comparatively more ephemeral—substance of hail). Indeed, "HEY your nails" stands on its own as a potentially self-contained line; as much of an exclamation as an end-punctuation-free poem can provide.

On the larger level of shape, there does not seem to be any formal consistency across Conrad's glitter-themed poems. For example, while "OBLIVIOUS IMPERIALISM" contains short lines of somewhat varied length, "Glitter in My Wounds" is a concrete poem, with its lines strictly arranged into angled and straight edges. The latter poem therefore does perform a kind of containment, though one that ultimately speaks to the formlessness and slipperiness of glitter. As poet Maria Sledmere—whose work displays similar entrancement with glitter as well as bubbles and foam—pointed out to me, glitter takes the shape of whatever container it fills, but "something always escapes." She therefore thinks of Conrad's poetry as invoking the "constant frustration inherent to glitter because it has these many forms and possibilities; it almost resists . . . a strict 'poetics' identifiable by specific formal tendencies."

Finally, the triple repetition of "glamour" (or "GLAMOUR") alongside "glitter[ed]" in "OBLIVIOUS IMPERIALISM" invites us to recognize the multitude of gl- words signifying brightness or sparkle, whether literally or metaphorically: "glare," "gleam," "glimmer," "glint," "glisten," "glister," "glitz," and "gloss."[6] Even the vocabulary of brightness and sparkle is excessive, just like its aesthetic.

Recall another poem, the late-14th-century's *Sir Gawain & the Green Knight*, which features glitter's first recorded usage in English: "And al watz rayled on red ryche golde naylez, / Þat al glytered and glent as glem of þe sunne"—"And all was arrayed with rich red gold nails, that all glittered and glinted as gleam of the sun." As my colleague Rowan Deer quipped, "check out that aglitteration!" And if we really wanted to be excessive here, we might throw yet another gl- word, "glitch," into the mix, at Sledmere's suggestion. She told me she thinks of "glitter as a moment of attention," a "kind of interruption, glitching"—which Conrad captures so well through those sporadic all-caps words.

Just as glitter recurs throughout Conrad's work, so do bubbles. In "Power Sissy Intervention #1: Queer Bubbles"— the transcription of their ritual notes, which produced a separate poem—Conrad recounts standing on a street corner in Asheville, North Carolina, blowing bubbles at children and announcing to their accompanying parents, "These bubbles will assure that your child will grow up to be a healthy, happy, revolutionary Queer who will help rid the world of homophobia, misogyny, racism, and other forms of stupidity."[7] Scholar Emma Train observes that Conrad's action "subverts a homophobic discourse of contagion and disease through its most literal enactment: that queer touch and queer proximity produces a queer identity . . . Conrad's bubbles matter queerness."[8] Put a different way, Conrad does not deny the notion of spreading queerness, but rather revalues it.

Similarly, glitter's champions understand that that substance connects marginalized people in positive ways—while others would align it with everything from a proliferating pollutant to a contagious virus. The similarities between glitter and bubbles are in fact extensive: both are colorful and visually interesting (bubbles, more specifically, are iridescent); both are aggregate objects (it's hard to blow just one bubble, much as it is hard to isolate just one piece of glitter); both move through the air; and both spark joy and create magical atmospheres, as I discuss further in Chapter 5. While, as I suggest there, glitter might be interchangeable with objects such as feathers, here Conrad shows us how bubbles might also function as glitter. The feelings and effects that such objects produce are more important than their actual composition. It therefore seems right to end on a few lines from Sledmere—who, in her 2021 poem "Foam Theory," alludes to those feelings and effects and, more specifically, to the ability of such objects to distort, and thereby provide relief from, our painful, workaday existence:

> . . . a decorative attitude to life itself
> keeps circling, circling.
> Each bubble will process the world's info
> thrice in shimmer.[9]

3 "TOO MUCH BLING"

GLITTER IN CHILDREN'S ENTERTAINMENT

"Animation is creating something that the human mind would want to believe but is seldom what would physically actually happen. There's a lot of psychology involved."

—YOUXI WOO[1]

While so far I have focused on glitter's real-world appearances, this substance also has a vivid fictional life, especially when it comes to children's entertainment. Recently, animated TV shows and films such as *Peppa Pig* (Astley Baker Davies Ltd., 2004-), *Spies in Disguise* (Blue Sky Studios, 2019), *DreamWorks Trolls* (2016), *DreamWorks Trolls World Tour* (2020), and illustrated books such as Angela DiTerlizzi and

Samatha Cotterill's *Just Add Glitter* (Beach Lane Books, 2018) have featured this substance prominently. These works manage to appeal to children as well as parents by figuring glitter as both enticing and obnoxious. They use glitter to subtly allude to anxieties over gender, bodily functions, and other issues, while also managing anxiety over glitter itself.

It's not surprising that we would find glitter in children's entertainment, given how its fun, frivolous aspects code it as youthful or at least immature. Further, as philosopher Thomas Leddy observes, "[v]ery young children are attracted more strongly to bright colours, shiny things, glitter, and the sparkle effects of marbles, soap-bubbles, kaleidoscopes, etc."[2] Of course, so are many adults. As I type this, I am wearing shiny plastic magenta eyeglass frames, a face mask with multi-colored tassels, a neon orange- and yellow-striped sweater, blue and white polka-dotted socks, and bright red sneakers.

But children's attraction to sparkle and shine is interesting in terms of its broader implications. Given that this attraction is found as early as infancy—when one has yet to internalize cultural associations such as, say, shininess=wealth—scientists believe that there is something primal and innate about it, probably stemming from our instinctive desire for water.[3] As Maria Sledmere quips, "Survival underlies glitter's aesthetic attraction."[4] (More cheekily, cabaret performer John Jarboe jested to me about her use of glitter, "I'm just trying to make people thirsty."[5]) In this sense, one might argue that people turn against sparkle and shine only once they encounter the cultural scripts I surveyed earlier, such as homophobia, heteronormativity, racism, and classism. Or perhaps just when they become the ones to have to clean it up. As the first line of A.E. Stallings' 2018 poem "Glitter" ruefully observes, "You have a daughter now. It's everywhere."[6]

It's also not surprising that something as vivid and vibrant as glitter would lend itself to modes such as animation and illustration. But as we will see, glitter actually poses some representational challenges to those modes—figuratively echoing the literal ways in which glitter proves difficult to capture.

Glitter Battles

Peppa Pig, the long-running British animated program for preschool-aged children, includes at least two episodes that voice cultural truisms about glitter's unruliness. In "School Project" and "Masks," we witness a struggle between parents and teachers on the one side and children on the other. As Peppa builds a castle for the titular school project in the first episode (actually, her parents are building it for her, in a subtle indictment of domestic labor that viewing parents will no doubt get and appreciate), she declares that she needs to put glitter on it. Mummy Pig and Daddy Pig (voiced by Morwenna Banks and Richard Ridings) nervously mumble excuses: "we've um . . . completely run out of glitter."[7] In the other episode, when Peppa's teacher Madame Gazelle (also voiced by Banks) tasks Peppa and her classmates with creating their own masks, she offers them "cardboard and colored paper, crayons, and paints, feathers, pipe cleaners, buttons, [and] pom poms," but draws the line at a request for glitter. The children (animals?) begin to chant, in what I find to be adorable British accents, "Glittah! Glittah! Glittah!" Again, Madame Gazelle refuses: "No! Glitter gets everywhere. There is no getting rid of it once it comes out. It is a menace."[8] My dear friend Sarah Pierce Waters, a former art teacher in Louisville, Kentucky, confirms these sentiments: "Art teachers HATE glitter. Kids lose their minds around glitter. They shake it everywhere, they can't stop."

While my friend held firm with her students, those in *Peppa Pig* finally wear their teacher down. Madame Gazelle, key in hand, approaches a blue door with two yellow triangular warning signs. Behind the door is a brick wall with an inlaid metal safe which she opens to reveal a small, glowing vial of glitter—playfully invoking the notion of glitter as toxic as well as vibrant. After Madame Gazelle issues a warning to the children about using this glitter carefully, the program cuts to a shot of parents arriving for afternoon pickup. The editing here encourages us to expect the worst (or best, depending on your opinion), which is soon realized: "Ah! Glitter!" Daddy Pig yelps, having opened the classroom door to be assaulted by a white cloud filled with colorful particles. "Don't panic, please remain calm," Madame Gazelle assures the parents. "There was a glitter leak but we have it under control now." She pulls out a vacuum cleaner and begins sucking the particles off Daddy Pig's sweater. Ultimately, the program responds to the intergenerational struggle over glitter by essentially shrugging, "Kids will be kids."

The feature-length animated film *Spies in Disguise* stages the struggle over glitter as one between different kinds of masculinity. We first meet Walter Beckett (voiced by Tom Holland) as a child, working on a gadget that will create a "glitter cloud" to make "bad guys leave you alone." Trying to understand his logic, his mother asks, "Because glitter makes people happy?" "Because the refracted light causes the enterochromaffin cells to release serotonin," he answers. She looks skeptical. "Yeah, glitter makes people happy," he concedes.[9] Surprisingly, the film depicts this boy's interest in glitter as persisting into manhood; the film cuts to several years later, when debonair super-spy Lance Sterling (voiced by Will Smith) finds himself caught in a dangerous mission and geeky Walter, now working as an inventor for the same spy agency, remotely deploys the glitter cloud gadget—since refined to create a cloud of pink glitter featuring holograms of kittens—and enables Lance to escape.

But Lance is a glitter skeptic at best. Returning to the agency office after his mission, he steps into the elevator and straightens up his suit lapels. As glitter puffs out—again, evoking its vibrancy and mobility—he grumbles, "Someone's gonna get it." After Lance begrudgingly partners with Walter for future missions, we watch him slowly come around from his macho ways—"Can't save the world with a hug," he insisted previously—to Walter's cutesy, non-violent solutions.

In addition to the aforementioned "kitty glitter," Walter deploys an inflatable "hug" that wraps itself around weapons and enemies, and something he calls both "yay-palm" and "50 shades of yay": plumes of smoke in different colors of the rainbow that envelop and disorient the bad guys.[10]

Lance's character arc mirrors that of Branch (voiced by Justin Timberlake) from DreamWorks Animation's feature *Trolls*. Unlike his fellow creatures, who spend their time hugging and dancing and singing, he tells the film's protagonist Poppy (voiced by Anna Kendrick) that he doesn't "do happy." We therefore have to laugh when Poppy pulls out a pop-up party invitation that shoots glitter onto his face; Lance and Branch act as the classic "straight men" whose seriousness in the context of frivolity makes them the butt of the joke.[11] (Speaking of butts, rear ends get a fair amount of airtime in *Trolls*, as we'll see shortly.) Like Lance, Branch eventually comes around. In this way, *Spies* and *Trolls* enact for males a similar experience that media scholar Michele White has described for females: "Glitter is a form of growing sideways [rather than up] because it is associated with wishes for more pleasure, leisure, and luxury."[12] In the case of *Spies* and *Trolls*, glitter is associated with wishes for happiness, kindness, and non-violence— supposedly childish mindsets that the two films affirm as valid worldviews for grown males.[13]

DiTerlizzi and Cotterill's *Just Add Glitter* demonstrates comparatively more anxiety about glitter. "Is there such a thing as *too much* bling? Depends on how much bling you bring," ponders the inside of the book's jacket. The book, which is targeted at 4-8-year-olds, introduces us to an unnamed little girl who likes to make crafts; as the text reads, "Try a speck, a fleck, a sprinkle. See how things begin to twinkle. A little here, a little there. Glitter, glitter, anywhere!" But soon, the girl and her cat are up to their necks in the substance, both looking concerned. "Uh-oh. STOP. We've got enough. We're *lost* in all this sparkly stuff," the text tells us.[14] Finally, we see the little girl sweeping a path through the glitter, while the text reflects, "I thought we needed all this bling, but it's too much of a good thing. The glitter made it hard to see, what sparkles most . . . is you and me."

Unlike *Spies* and *Trolls*, *Just Add Glitter* suggests that children, and in this particular case, girls, eventually need to grow up, not sideways—which entails putting away childish (sparkling) things. But somewhat ironically, this book features a cover and multiple pages encrusted with real glitter; the book's cover also boasts, "With glitter on every page!" That is, while the narrative seems to warn against too much of this substance—because it enacts excessive femininity? because it entails waste and overconsumption? it's never really clear—the physical book itself trades on attraction to glitter. And in fact, one could complain that the cautionary narrative doesn't really match the gleeful permissiveness suggested by the title *Just Add Glitter*. But rather than accusing this work of inconsistency or even hypocrisy, we could say that it simply articulates one of glitter's many paradoxes, namely its status as a source of both anxiety and joy.

The Challenge of Capturing Glitter

While *Just Add Glitter* simply affixes the substance in question to its cover and pages, animated works for children face unique challenges when it comes to representing glitter—in part because animation cannot represent this substance as realistically as photographic media theoretically can. But, as I will show, these works devise creative solutions to these representational challenges. In fact, the artistic freedom of animation allows these works to enhance and, in some cases, even fabricate—in emotionally resonant ways—the properties of glitter, including how it moves and sounds.

In both "School Project" and "Masks," *Peppa Pig*'s animators render glitter animate by playing with color. A given piece of glitter on Suzy Sheep's dress switches continually back and forth from yellow to green, while another switches continually back and forth from blue to white, thereby creating a flickering effect. This creative choice highlights glitter's real-life qualities of being dynamic and changeable—its ability, depending on composition, to reflect light. *Peppa*'s solution to animating glitter reminds me of the assertion of 5-year-old Rory, my friend Kate Wright's son, that he likes glitter because it "has sparkles" that are "shiny . . . like a heart." When she asked him to elaborate, he explained, "it's like the heart like beeping . . . because it goes shiny and then it doesn't go shiny . . . and that is like a beat."

Trolls and *Trolls World Tour* are comparatively more ambitious undertakings than *Peppa Pig*. According to visual effects supervisor Matt Baer, "'Glitter is a tricky thing to capture in terms of what each of those little mirrored surfaces are doing.'"[15] Visual effects lead Youxi Woo explained to me further that, "If we 'set the rule'" within the computer animation software "that the glitter would reflect *everything* then we would be granted [a] more realistic [look], but would also inherit the reflection when we did not necessarily want it."[16] For example, "Glitter Troll" Guy Diamond encounters other characters such as Branch and Poppy, who are furry and colorful (pink and dark aqua, respectively). Therefore, each individual glitter piece on Guy's body could be reflecting multiple fibers and colors in every frame—which, with 24 image frames per second, would look quite distracting. Woo adds that "there is the additional cost of having [glitter] reflect everything—the more you reflect, the longer the computer takes to calculate the colors, and the more expensive your film becomes"—an interesting point that speaks to glitter's debatable cheapness, discussed in the last chapter. In short, glitter onscreen would end up looking "too noisy," per Woo, if it were designed as truly reflective.[17]

Another issue the *Trolls* animators ran into was animating facial expressions for the "Glitter Troll" characters. Woo explained to me that creating a character in 3D animation typically entails "wrap[ping] a stretchable image over the character as its skin," a process that he compared to draping a piece of cloth over someone. Following this analogy, the "cloth" will bend and stretch along with the character, especially when it comes to the face and mouth, as with smiling or frowning. The problem, as Woo pointed out, is that, with a "'glitter design,' we understand inherently that glitter is hard plastic and should not stretch. So if it does, we subconsciously feel that it is not right, and is not glitter."[18] The solution, according to Baer, was "'to build and improve our glitter shader'"—the "'shader,'" in this case, being the set of instructions fed to the piece of software that renders the final image—"'to analyze the amount of stretching [and then] refer back to an object frame or reference frame,'" in order to keep the glitter from looking too stretched.[19]

For *Trolls World Tour*, DreamWorks animators embarked on what Woo referred to as "the next step [in the] expansion of glitter functionality": building "an entire environment full of glitter."[20] The animators were tasked with creating a "glitter desert," replete with wind flurries, in which the character Cooper (voiced by Ron Funches), finds himself stranded. As Woo and Doug Rizeakos explain, they wanted to blend "the visual expectations of a sand-filled desert with the physical nature of flattened glitter pieces"—a contradiction insofar as grains of sand are spherical, not flat, and in that "glitter, on the whole, doesn't move, stack, or shape itself like sand." Further, glitter/sand particles are larger in relation to Trolls, as the *Trolls*verse imagines them, than they would be to a human, so the animators had to think about how to represent scale accordingly. The animators met these challenges by, among

FIGURE 2 A "glitter desert" in *Trolls World Tour*. DreamWorks Trolls © 2021 DreamWorks Animation LLC. All Rights Reserved.

other things, "develop[ing] mathematical procedures to integrate with various simulation techniques" and building custom software.[21] Once again, the problem of glitter is eventually solved—it's captured, at least by some standards of satisfaction—through a great deal of creative labor and technological innovation.

Moving Glitter: Physics, Sound, and Emotion

In these examples of children's entertainment, glitter is often in motion: bursting from doorways; being flung into faces; pouring out of watering cans; flowing from showerheads; and streaming from butts, as we will soon see. Which raises questions of physics or, rather, fictional physics. That is, these works imagine capacities for glitter that it doesn't technically have—a move that is of course enabled by animation's relative detachment from realism. In this way, we might think in terms of animation's unique capacities rather than its possible limitations. Indeed, as scholar Nicole Starosielski argues, this mode "should not be considered secondary to indexical forms" such as documentary or news media, "but instead as providing views difficult to achieve" with those forms, including emotional or ideological views.[22]

For example, in the "Masks" episode of *Peppa Pig* wherein Daddy Pig opens the classroom door, colorful glitter bursts forth in a white cloud as if it were a gas that had been trapped inside a small space—thereby capturing parents' perceptions of this substance as overwhelming and (ob)noxious. In *Spies in Disguise*, when young Walter demonstrates his glitter-explosion gadget to his mother, the pieces of glitter hang in the air and fall slowly, like snow. This depiction provides a nice segue to the next scene, which finds present-day Lance ascending a Japanese mountain under snowfall.

As different as the contexts may be, we could compare this treatment in *Spies* to a sequence in the acclaimed 2017 French film *120 BPM (Beats per Minute)*, centered on AIDS activists in 1990s Paris. The sequence in question employs slow motion, allowing us to focus on the large pieces of glitter falling around the characters during a Pride parade, thanks to a glitter cannon. The enchantment, pleasure, effervescence, and lightheartedness that the characters in this scene experience are both represented and occasioned by glitter.[23]

(I should also mention that the protagonist is on drugs in this scene—not so much a children's film!—so he's feeling that same slow lightness that the glitter possesses.) In both *Spies in Disguise* and *120 BPM*, artistic license around the actual motion of glitter captures its accompanying emotions.

Likewise, these children's works are interested in imagining how glitter *sounds*, a pursuit that broadens what we primarily think of as a visual phenomenon. (In the next chapter, we will consider how glitter tastes as well as feels, in the tactile sense. In fact, it seems as if smell is the only one of the five senses that glitter does not activate, fictionally or otherwise.) That first depiction of a glitter explosion from *Spies in Disguise* is accompanied by whooshing and then whimsical tinkling sounds, almost like wind chimes; as the pieces in the air grow fewer, the sounds grow quieter. When Daddy Pig opens that classroom door in "Masks," we hear a kind of rushing "vooom" sound, similarly followed by tinkling. And in "School Project," when Suzy Sheep arrives to her classroom with her mother and her "fairy palace" in tow, we hear a sand-like sifting sound as the glitter spills onto the floor—which brings to my mind a meme a friend once shared with me: "Glitter is just sand that majored in musical theatre."[24] As an analog book, diTerlizzi and Cotterill's *Just Add Glitter* obviously cannot capture sound directly. But it does feature rhymes—recall the point about "how much bling you bring"—that chime with glitter's playful associations. And the term "bling" is itself quite interesting in terms of sound. New Orleans-based rapper B.G. reportedly coined this "vibraphonic" word in 1998 "to characterize 'the sound light makes as it hits a diamond.'"[25]

Of course, no such sound actually exists. But it *feels* as if it does. Likewise, someone who finds glitter mesmerizing might experience it as falling as slowly as snow. While I suppose a great deal of moving glitter might actually make the shifting-sand sound described above, it would certainly not be as prominent in real life as in *Peppa Pig*. And obviously glitter makes no sound whatsoever in many if not most situations, such as sitting atop a greeting card—unless you're talking about the "Glitter" ringtone available on the Samsung Galaxy Smartphone, in which case it sounds like five tinkly notes (C-G-C-C-G) that decrescendo, not unlike how glitter falls after being thrown in the air. These creative reinterpretations allow us to explore the emotions and ideas that an object like glitter inspires, highlighting its unique appeal.

Seeing and Not Seeing Glitter

In many of these examples, glitter functions paradoxically as at once hyper-visual and as a deterrent to seeing. We've heard how, in *Spies in Disguise*, glitter serves as a distraction that allows Lance and Walter to elude captors. In *Trolls*, it similarly disorients the bad guys, like a gentler, prettier kind of Mace. When the Trolls are being held captive by a scullery maid in an evil king's palace, Guy Diamond (voiced by Kunal

Nayyar) twirls and shoots a bunch of glitter from his bare butt into her face. (A Wiki page on the franchise informs us that Glitter Trolls "prefer to be completely naked."[26]) "Glitter! No!" the maid yells—echoing the parents and teacher of Peppa Pig—as the Trolls escape. And later, when a hideous dog-like creature is chasing the Trolls around the palace, Poppy commands, "Diamond, glitter him!" Guy obliges, as seen in the following image, releasing another sparkly plume into the creature's face while shouting, "Eat glitter!"

Guy's ability to "poop" or "fart" glitter, along with his battle cry of "Eat glitter!", makes a strange link between glitter and both excretion and ingestion.[27] As we will see later in this book, the marketing of glitter foods and beers picks up on the notion of ingestion; people do, indeed, eat and drink glitter, though usually of their own volition. Meanwhile,

FIGURE 3 Guy Diamond to the rescue in *Trolls*. DreamWorks Trolls © 2021 DreamWorks Animation LLC. All Rights Reserved.

some have taken to imagining glitter and excretion in a negative direction. For example, US photographer Hannah Altman has used glitter to stand in for tears, vomit, and menstrual blood in a photo series titled "And Everything Nice."[28] Walking the middle ground between ingestion and excretion, an article from Florida Gulf Coast University warns that each "piece of glitter that has been tossed or blown skyward in pursuit of the perfect [graduation] celebration picture . . . still sits in the bowels of our 800-acre campus"—a curiously constipated image, compared to Guy Diamond's butt capacities.[29]

But in children's entertainment it seems as if glitter serves as a more charming way to talk about (unblocked) bodily processes. And indeed, research suggests that kids are obsessed with poop and fart jokes in large part because they allow them to work through their anxieties over lack of bodily control.[30] (I can't speak for others, but I would vastly prefer to have an "accident" that involved pooping glitter rather than pooping actual poop.) Young *Trolls* fans might therefore be tickled, as I was, to learn about the Brooklyn trend of street artists glittering unsightly dog poop on public sidewalks.[31]

Thinking of glitter and the (un)sightly in this way brings us to another fascinating anecdote about glitter's (in)visibility: the "Great Glitter Mystery" introduced by Caity Weaver in *The New York Times* in 2018. From Weaver's exchange with a spokesperson for Glitterex, a major glitter manufacturer:

When I asked Ms. Dyer if she could tell me which industry served as Glitterex's biggest market, her answer was instant: "No, I absolutely know that I can't." . . . I asked if she could tell me why she couldn't tell me. "Because they don't want anyone to know that it's glitter." "If I looked at it, I wouldn't know it was glitter?" "No, not really." "Would I be able to see the glitter?" "Oh, you'd be able to see something. But it's—yeah, I can't."[32]

The article prompted a Reddit "Unsolved Mysteries" thread with over 2,000 comments, many of which hypothesized that the industry is toothpaste, automotive paint, and/or boat manufacturing.[33] This mystery goes against the idea of glitter as hyper-visible; we *don't* always know it when we see it. Here, glitter becomes unexpectedly invisible, a secret ingredient in another substance or object.

We see such paradoxes around glitter's visual capacities in other contexts. The Internet beauty bloggers that Michele White has studied report that they can't stop staring at their fingernails when they paint them with glitter—but also joke about mesmerizing, confusing, or blinding themselves or others. Similarly, calling glitter a "technology of enchantment," Ph.D. student Parisa Ahmadi recalls her time working in the cosmetics industry: "[s]wiping product on the skin [and] watching it sparkle in a range of colors and prismatic refractions is hypnotic," often leaving customers with "gaping mouths."[34] Glitter, in short, feels like a break in reality, and from realistic perception specifically.[35] Consider glitter's close association with the verb "dazzle," which strangely means both "to shine brilliantly" and "to lose clear vision" in the intransitive form, according to *Merriam-Webster's Dictionary*. So: *His dress dazzled* or *I was dazzled*. The transitive form makes the double nature more clear: "to confound with brilliance."[36] So: *This book on glitter dazzled the reader*. Perhaps the Scottish Gaelic adjective "glamsy," which I learned when I moved to Edinburgh, is also useful here: "Of the sky—glittering, bright and dazzling in parts and very dark elsewhere."[37] Again, a paradox: is glitter a hyper-visual object, tied to sight? Or does it prevent seeing?

To return to the realm of fictional entertainment, Mariah Carey's 2001 star vehicle *Glitter* features a scene in which the titular substance rains down on the singer as a music video director pauses filming and shouts to the crew, "The glitter can't overpower the artist. Could we clean this up?"[38] Glitter "pulls focus," to use a film industry term, preventing us from seeing what (supposedly) really matters. Remember *Just Add Glitter*: "The glitter made it *hard to see*, what sparkles most . . . is you and me." No wonder this substance is perceived as frivolous.

In fact, despite their typical associations with illumination, clarity, and enlightenment, phenomena such as sparkle, shine, and light just as often obscure, as the phrase "blinded by the light" suggests. And sometimes literally, and tragically, so. At the risk of taking too gruesome a detour from cute Troll farts, we might recall the real-life case of a US woman who, in helping her daughter with a craft project, wound up with a piece of glitter in her eye that scratched her cornea and led to an infection and eventual loss of vision. Similar cautionary tales abound, such as that of a UK woman who was nearly blinded thanks to glitter from a Christmas card.[39]

Glitter has proven dangerous to other parts of the human body as well. In the "Matter of Amato v. R.R. Heywood Co., Inc." in 1960, a New York company lost its appeal against a worker's compensation claim. The worker was employed for 12 years "as foreman of [a] machine room where greeting cards were finished. . . . A substance called 'glitter' was used to decorate the greeting cards and it was determined that it was almost pure silica"—most likely, crystalline silica, known more commonly as quartz, which today can be found in sparkling kitchen and bathroom countertops. After a coughing attack, the claimant was diagnosed with silico-tuberculosis.[40] Today, silica is widely recognized as a carcinogen and construction workers and others who might be exposed to it must wear protective gear.

In this light, Walter's non-violent *Spies* methods take on quite a different sheen—as does the prospect of ingesting glitter. But again, we could say that children's entertainment serves to manage anxieties over glitter's (statistically rare) dangers. At the same time, glitter serves in these works to negotiate anxieties around phenomena ranging from gender roles to waste to the porousness and vulnerability of the body.

In riffing on the challenges of representing glitter in animation and illustration, I may have implied that photographic technologies are relatively superior when it comes to that task. But that may not be so. Some of the beauty bloggers that White studies use phrases such as, "photography doesn't do it justice"[41]—presumably in terms of glitter's visual effects, but also possibly in terms of its emotional ones. Further, even if a photograph manages to satisfactorily capture glitter (the noun), it cannot itself *glitter* (the verb). As my colleague Rowan Deer puts it: "glittering is a temporal, dynamic effect that happens between the light source, the observer and the glitter. Glitter plays on the movement of the wearer or watcher—a movement that is always arrested by a photograph." And this is true even when the "glitter" in question is not the commercial product. When walking home last winter, I naively pulled out my phone to try to capture the glints of light winking up at me from the snowbanks alongside the Munich sidewalk. No dice.

But in any case, these animated and illustrated works of children's entertainment are particularly unique when it comes to representing glitter. We could see them as "meta" or self-referential, whether intentionally or not: they present narrative content about glitter's physically ungraspable or unruly nature at the same time that they struggle to capture it formally. And these works dramatize how glitter makes it hard to see, just as their real-life creators find it hard to represent it visually. These works therefore turn away from objective reality and imagine glitter through subjective experience.

Having spent four years and counting working on this book, I certainly relate to these artistic struggles to capture glitter. I can only hope that, here, I have conceptually captured a few flecks.

Interview: Machine Dazzle

In December 2018 I attended *Holiday Sauce* at my alma mater UCLA's Royce Hall: a festive show from performer Taylor Mac, the MacArthur "genius" grant-winner who uses the gender pronoun "judy." judy sported glitter on judy's eyelids, eyebrows, lips, and cheeks—chiming with the tinsel, tulle, beads, baubles, sequins, and Christmas ornaments comprising judy's outrageously elaborate costume. I witnessed

FIGURE 4 Taylor Mac's *Holiday Sauce* produced by Pomegranate Arts and Nature's Darlings. Taylor Mac's costume by Machine Dazzle. Presented on December 14, 2018 by UCLA's Center for the Art of Performance. Photo by Reed Hutchinson. (Author on the right.)

all this up close, having been randomly summoned on stage and given a shot of whiskey along with a dozen or so other folks who also knew the lyrics to The Pogues' bawdy holiday hymn, "Fairytale of New York." My hand was shaking so badly with stage fright that I spilled at least half of the whiskey. It was probably the highlight of my entire life.

But the real star of the show was, arguably, neither Mac nor me but costume designer Machine Dazzle, who made a cameo as a towering Christmas tree draped in tinsel garlands. Winner of a 2017 Henry Hewes Design Award, Dazzle fashioned several other fabulous ensembles for *Holiday Sauce* and has collaborated extensively with Mac and other creative figures. When I asked Dazzle in June 2021 if he would be willing to do an interview for this book he said, "Let's make it happen. I'm a bit crazed, but glitter is a necessary body part."

NS: *What are your pronouns?*
MD: He/him/hey
I read somewhere that your motto is, "Glitter rhymes with litter! Get into it!" [42] *In that spirit of excess, could you elaborate?*
Glitter is magical in light, but it can also look cheap and it's bad for the environment.. all in all it's very entertaining.
You've led a "trashion" workshop using recycled materials, and it looks like a lot of your costumes involve reclaimed materials in some way as well. So, that motto

notwithstanding, would you say that your work is eco-minded in some way, or at least committed to a version of recycling?

I'm eco friendly for the most part. I love found objects, recycled things.. My use of reclaimed items is two part.. I love the aesthetic and I have to be budget conscious. I do recycle and pick from my own recycling bin all the time!

Is there a costume or outfit from history that has inspired your work?

Forever, the flip flop dress from *Priscilla, Queen of The Desert*! It was just so fun, easy, fresh, hilarious, sculptural, and was a bit shocking yet totally appropriate for the moment.

The famous "Proust Questionnaire" includes the query, "What is your greatest extravagance?" But your aesthetic is already all about extravagance, so I want to ask you the inverse: what is your greatest prudence? What do you find yourself skimping on or cutting back on? What do we need less of in the world?

I think my maximalist approach comes off as extravagant.. but really instead of an embarrassment of riches (because it isn't) it's more like an experiment of ideas..

because that's how I work.. I dress Taylor in ideas.. but the answer.. what the world needs less of is stock costumes.. what I mean by that is, the assumed or typical costume for certain kinds of characters..

I still think about that incredible costume you designed for Holiday Sauce, *pictured here. If that outfit could talk, what would she say?*

Naughty or Nice? You decide, Cackle!!

4 RECRAFTING GLITTER

THE SUSTAINABLE TURN

I'm sorry that the haters don't like fun. I love fun, and my favorite color is sparkle.

—CAT WIEST, professional brewer and creator of "Mermaid Tale Ale" glitter beer

Canadian blogger and mechanical engineer Debbie Chapman authored a blog post in 2016 offering to teach readers "How to Make Homemade Glitter" by simply adding food coloring to one of three possible substances: sugar (presumably sucrose, consisting of carbon, hydrogen, and oxygen), "regular salt" (presumably sodium and chloride plus possible additives), or Epsom salt (magnesium, sulfur, and oxygen), then sun-drying or baking. Chapman enthuses, alluding to (plastic) glitter's negative reputation as well as its craft usage, "It sticks to glue just like regular glitter but it is sooooo much easier to clean up!"—presumably because sugar and salt granules are heavier and thicker than your average piece of craft glitter.

Chapman's post, perhaps unwittingly, revises commonplace definitions of "glitter." In her version, many of the qualities that we have seen assigned to glitter—including irritation, dispersal, and persistence—have fallen away. Apparently, anything can be called glitter as long as it is colorful, decorative, sparkly, and particulate.[1] And perhaps even sparkle and particulation don't matter that much: sugar and salt are shiny but not as reflective as classic glitter due to a lack of aluminum. And sugar glitter, apparently, "clumps" up. But Chapman reminds us that you "can even put it on cupcakes!"[2]

This book will conclude with a look at what such a revision means in a global context where plastic has become "a pervasive condition."[3] But first, let us explore the widening world of what we might sum up as "ecoglitter": products or additives designed to be edible, biodegradable, sustainable, and/or ethical. Ecoglitter complicates the current narrative of glitter as a pernicious pollutant, while reminding us of the longer history of natural objects and substances that we might categorize as glitter. At the same time, ecoglitter enacts the intersection of seemingly-opposed impulses—namely, queer frivolity and environmental sustainability.

Eat, Drink, and Be "Shim-Merry": Ingesting Glitter

The glitter cupcakes that Chapman references are just one of the many sparkly foodstuffs that have recently captured the Western imagination. Considering that "sparkle and shine are associated with cheerfulness," it's not surprising that edible glitter appears across those indulgent categories of desserts and treats, dusting macarons, cake pops, and donuts.[4] But one can also order glitter gravy from the Fox under the Hill pub in Greenwich, UK during the winter holidays—or order your own packet from a company called PopaBall to ensure a "Shim-Merry Christmas."[5] The Santa Monica, California-based restaurant Dagwoods serves a "Magical AF [as Fuck] Pizza" topped with edible glitter, which received a ribbing from US late-night talk show host Jimmy Kimmel. Dagwoods' Instagram thanked Kimmel for the attention, "even if [the pizza] does make you want to burn our restaurant to the ground"—a presumably tongue-in-check invocation of the hatred that many people feel for glitter.[6] While the other pizzas on Dagwoods' menu are represented by straightforward photographs—even their fried Spam and pineapple pie—the entry for this particular pizza features a whimsical 1960s-esque font and a cartoon of a unicorn vomiting a rainbow. It thereby activates glitter's associations with countercultures, the infantile, and, by way of the unicorn, the magical and the queer.[7]

Items like glitter gravy and the Magical AF Pizza are especially attention-grabbing because these savory dishes are not, in their typical form, coded as frivolous and feminized the way sweet treats and desserts are. Further, in the case of the pizza, the earthy and primary color scheme of the dish—the ecru of cheese and the crimson of tomatoes—doesn't seem to jibe with the shimmering tertiary tones of aqua, pink, and purple that adorn it. Perhaps this chromatic dissonance adds to the sense of these items as unnatural; as not fit for consumption. Consider scholar and former US national park ranger Jennifer Ladino's rumination on the color schemes that we think of as natural or environmental, and how they connect to specific emotions: "the ranger uniform," like national park signage, "blends aesthetically with the natural landscape. Both are 'olive-drab,' with a nuance that's easy to miss. . . . [T]he tone of the [uniforms and] signage matches the solemn, historical mood of the site."[8] And yet, all the colors of the rainbow exist in nature—as anyone who's ever seen the Northern Lights (aurora borealis) or bright pink plumeria flowers or a neon tetra fish or a flame bowerbird can attest.

The popularity of glitter foods and their kin is no doubt driven by social media's emphasis on documenting new or zeitgeist-y experiences—"do it for the 'gram," as the kids say—and by a 24-hour news cycle that grants airtime to such arguably inconsequential matters. Additionally, the color and sparkle of these products dovetail nicely with social media's insistence on the visual. And, of course, the intentionally-limited availability of many of these products also drives their popularity. (The glitter-adjacent "Unicorn Frappuccino" from Starbucks lasted for only one bright and shining week. I blinked and missed it.) And thanks to the links between LGBTQ+ communities and glitter, as well as rainbows and unicorns, many glitter foods and drinks are linked to Pride events, which typically take place once a year in June. But the Magical AF Pizza is an exception: it prompted so many requests that Dagwoods brought it back the next year, "and ha[s] no plans to take it off the menu." General manager Mark Peters told *TimeOut* magazine, "'It's outrageously popular . . . You should see how happy some of these kids are—but really, people of all ages.'"[9] Here, we see the outsized pleasure, matched by the outsized *dis*pleasure, that people take in glitter.

The title of the aforementioned *TimeOut* article on glitter pizza is, "We've Gone Too Far." And the direction we've gone is backwards, if we are to believe thinkers such as our old fiend Adolph Loos, author of the very subtly titled 1913 essay, "Ornament and Crime," which claimed that "*The evolution of culture is synonymous with the removal of ornament from utilitarian objects*."[10] Of course, aestheticizing food is nothing new, as, for example, the traditional Thai art of fruit carving attests. And some categories of food serve primarily aesthetic purposes, as Colin Nissan reminds us in his enduringly funny October 2009 essay for *McSweeney's*, "It's Decorative Gourd Season, Motherfuckers." But whereas processes like fruit carving make art *out of* food, glitter dishes entail adding art *to* food. And if glitter is understood as decorative and therefore unnecessary, and food is sustentative and therefore necessary, then there is something counter-instinctual about ingesting glitter—especially considering its dominant association with plastic. ("No, you do not pee or shit glitter" after ingesting it, US glitter-beer brewer Cat Wiest sighed when we chatted. "I often joke that if I ever pass a kidney stone it may look like an Easter Egg though.") Ironically, each of us eats, drinks, and/or inhales up to 74,000 particles of microplastics every year; we are ingesting non-organic material constantly.[11] And yet that factoid has not had the same viral life as the previously-discussed Great Glitter Backlash.

Indeed, the rush to dust one's food with sparkle has raised the concern of at least one governing body, the US Food and Drug Administration (FDA). In 2018, having become aware that "some non-edible decorative glitters and dusts are promoted for use on foods," the FDA released a formal statement clarifying that edible products are required by law to include a list of ingredients on their labels. Officially-edible glitters—which might contain cornstarch, maltodextrin, gum Arabic, carnauba wax, titanium dioxide, iron oxide, mica, and/or color additives—bear the notation "Edible." "Non-Toxic" or "For Decorative Purposes Only" does not make the grade. Strangely, then, if a product contains something deemed not-so-great for you to eat, such as plastic, it will *not* be listed.

But categories such as "edible" are rather arbitrary. As a child, I was fascinated by the jar of silver dragées that my mother kept in the cupboard for holiday cookie decorating. I got to enjoy a good 24 years of those incredibly hard, shiny, tiny balls before they were banned in my home state of California thanks to a 2003 lawsuit; residents of the other 49 states can still go wild. (Turns out, ingesting silver in extremely large quantities—so, absolute boatloads of dragées—can trigger an outlandish but very real condition known as argyria, in which one's skin turns permanently blue and kidney function and night vision are potentially disrupted.) In 2014, a UK woman was convicted under food safety laws for selling glitter made of plastic shavings to cake companies under the dodgy name EdAble Art Ltd.[12] But apparently, no one died or was even sickened by her shenanigans. And I've yet to hear of any other industries or companies being held to account for those 74,000 particles of microplastics that we inadvertently consume every year. These vignettes show us that edibility and decoration are not only matters of taste, both literally and figuratively, but also of legal interpretation.

What pairs well with glitter pizza, you ask? Why, a glitter beer, of course. Alex Nowell of California's Three Weavers Brewing Company has been credited with launching this craze in 2015 with "Mel's Sparkle Pony," a pink West Coast IPA made with hibiscus. A multitude of breweries have since followed suit.[13] "Cosmic Fog" by Utah's Strap Tank Brewery is a fruity sour that is both glittery and purple, thanks to butterfly pea flower. Maryland's DuClaw Brewing Company teamed up with Diablo Doughnuts in 2019 to make "Sour Me

Unicorn Farts," another sour brewed with tangerines, limes, and cherries, plus Fruity Pebbles cereal added into the mash. (I personally have tried three other takes on glitter beer, as you can see in the following "Taste Test.")

Going gluten-free? You might satisfy your glitter-drink yearnings with Goldschläger, the Swiss cinnamon liqueur filled with thin flakes of real gold. (Upon trying it in college, I wisecracked that "it tastes like it's Christmas and someone's trying to kill me.") Or for a classier touch, buy some pure gold or silver powder at 23 karats or higher and make a "Golden Negroni" like that served at Supernova in Munich, Germany—consisting of Tanqueray gin, Belsazar white vermouth, lemon bitters, gentian root liqueur, and tiny gold sparkles.

Like me, Jeff Alworth—US beer guru and founder of the blog *Beervana*—was left "smitten" by his first encounter with the glitter beer trend a few years ago. After posting about it on social media, he was "surprised to see it spark intense reactions across the board. Glitter," he concluded, "gets people talking." But not always positively. The blog *American Craft Beer*, in a "Bad Ideas in Brewing" column on the trend, opined, "Glitter is similar to confetti . . . or sequins (. . . other items we hope don't start showing up in beer)."[14] Speak for yourself!

Men in particular responded quite negatively to Alworth's glitter beer posts, "scoffing [that] it was 'gimmicky'—even though," as he points out, "the current white-hot fad in beer, hazy IPA, is *entirely* based on appearance. (And it is beloved

FIGURE 5 Sour Me Unicorn Farts by DuClaw Brewing. Photo by Rachel Bradley.

by men . . .)." In fact, visual appearance has always been a factor in beer consumption; "the success of pilsner in the mid-19th century was due almost entirely to . . . people's ability to see it in the new transparent glasses that were becoming popular at the time."[15]

When I interviewed him, Alworth lamented that the "gendered thing is . . . not super shocking to me" because beer making and drinking "is a very masculine world." Add to that the fact that, as he reports, glitter beer's "main practitioners have been women," and it seems like we have just another classic manifestation of the associations previously discussed: glitter is considered feminine, the feminine is associated with the frivolous and obsession with appearance (despite masculine people's documented obsession with appearance), and then that misogynist and femme-phobic ideology gets turned against glittery objects.

And yet, brewer Cat Wiest testified that it was actually some women in the industry who "publicly shamed me for 'turning the clock back on women's progress' by putting glitter in beer. That really hurt my feelings," she confided to me. "What I did was make a great quality beer, and gave it another dimension in which to be enjoyed. People shop with their eyes, and when folks saw my glitter beer they would gasp and take photos; it was awesome!" When I asked her what the experience of making glitter beer has taught her, she said—eye-shoppers notwithstanding—"I learned that some people really really HATE glitter."

I'm Ready for My Glow-Up: Wearing Ecoglitter

Cosmetic glitter—found in products ranging from eyeshadow to nail polish to lipstick as well as in loose form—has often been made primarily out of microplastics. But now, in addition to your stomach lining, you can gild your external body parts in low- or no-plastic glitter, thanks to the dozens of wholesale manufacturers and individual brands that have sprung up in the last few years. So-called biodegradable glitters "predominately use regenerated cellulose or modified regenerated cellulose," sourced primarily from eucalyptus trees, "as their core" rather than plastic. Then, as with their conventional counterparts, that core is "coated with aluminium and/or mineral pigment for reflectivity and topped with a thin plastic layer (e.g. styrene acrylate)."[16]

UK-headquartered Bioglitter, a wholesaler that manu-factures in Germany and supplies to brands such as Projekt Glitter (Berlin) and BioGlitz (Los Angeles), has been making such low-plastic glitters for many years and recently unveiled a product known as "Cosmetic Bioglitter™ PURE": totally free of plastic as well as aluminum and carmine, and independently certified as biodegradable.[17] On a smaller scale, *RuPaul's Drag Race* alum Acid Betty has her own line of low-plastic, "biodegradable" glitter sprays and gels known as Unicorn Skin. (A minor drama broke out when she threw shade at fellow queen Trixie Mattel for her nonbiodegradable Trixie Cosmetics glitter.[18]) Brazil's family-owned and -operated Pura Bioglitter makes their no-plastic product from mica and agar-agar extracted from algae; they promise that it will "dissolve in water or compos[t] in just three days."[19] And even Meadowbrook Inventions, which invented commercial plastic glitter in 1934, now offers a no-plastic Bio-Jewels option.

Ecoglitter brands' commitment to sustainability tends to extend beyond the product itself to include packaging. For example, the ecoglitter line DAZZLE, released by UK art collective Culture Hustle, comes in 5 short cardboard cylinders for different colors, packed in a longer cardboard tube. Pura Bioglitter uses glass tubes with cork stoppers, while the UK's EcoStardust glitter sets come in recyclable metal tins inside a recyclable paper carton without plastic coating.[20]

Of course, any utopian visions of cosmetic ecoglitter should be tempered by further consideration. For one thing, low-plastic versions still contain up to 8% plastic, and their "biodegradable" claims might be misleading, considering that "only the core material of glitter (without the reflective coatings and sealants [or packaging, for that matter]) needs to be tested in order to be certified as 'biodegradable.'"[21] Scholar Vanbasten Noronha de Araújo also points out that "even biological matter can unsettle [an] ecosystem's functions if [it is] not properly introduced into the wider cycles of energy use."[22] In Cambridge, UK in 2021, the first-ever study of biodegradable glitter found that this substance still had environmental impacts in fresh water—such as reducing the root length of duckweed and increasing the presence of an invasive species, the New Zealand mud snail.[23] Further, de Araújo notes that mica, a non-renewable resource used in some but not all ecoglitter products, is often mined by child laborers.[24]

But glitter does not seem to be a significant pollutant, as described in Chapter 1. We might also note that some cosmetic manufacturers have begun replacing mica with synthetic mica, also known as synthetic fluorphlogopite, to address at least that labor issue. UK-based Lush Cosmetics pledged to do so starting in 2018 when they could no longer confirm that their supplier was sourcing mica ethically; today, their Web site features a statement on "Combating Modern Slavery."[25] Pura Bioglitter also uses lab-made mica. These brands therefore seem to understand "sustainability" not as a synonym for "natural," per se, but as a broad term that encompasses environmental and social responsibility.

In response to ecoglitter's possible imperfections, we might also adopt a stance against what some scholars have called "purity politics": the all-or-nothing mentality of much environmentalism that stymies action and innovation.[26] This might mean looking at the glass, or rather the glitter, as 92% plastic-free rather than 8% plastic-full. Or remembering that, as public thinkers such as Jenny Price have shown, the rush toward "sustainability" can sometimes lead to more wastefulness and consumerism than working within imperfect systems.[27] I was therefore impressed, rather than cynical, when I interviewed Projekt Glitter founder Jeanne Low in 2020; she told me that while she aims to switch to the 100% plastic-free glitter made by BioGlitter, she still has a lot of stock of the old, low-plastic glitter that she plans to finish selling first rather than throwing away. She also hinted at the economic difficulty of starting an eco-friendly business, explaining that she initially sold plastic container lids because Projekt Glitter was initially too small to meet the order minimums set by metal cap manufacturers. "[You] have to start somewhere . . . you can't be 100% green from the get-go," she observed.[28]

Glitter's recent eco-turn speaks to a much longer history of sparkly, shiny adornment drawn from nature. Given that sparkly minerals such as hematite and mica were used in prehistoric cave paintings, one could argue that glitter as an aesthetic phenomenon is at least 35,000 years old.[29] Cosmetic usage more specifically dates back to the earliest human civilizations, with cosmetic palettes uncovered from as early as 5,000 BCE.[30] Ancient Egyptian women "had at their disposal a whole rainbow of cosmetics, all of which were made from rocks, minerals, and plants in the region. Cleopatra . . . used a deep blue eye shadow with gold-colored pyrite flecks, made from ground lapis lazuli stone"[31]—which Egyptians obtained through trade with Afghanistan, where the stone has been abundant.[32] (A widely-circulated story also has it that Egyptians used ground-up iridescent beetles' wings as a cosmetic, but I have been unable to find any reliable source for this claim.[33]) In later periods such as the Renaissance, facial "glow"—a close cousin to sparkle and shine—was the order of the day. Historian Jill Burke told me that women hoped to achieve this effect with, among other things, moisturizers made of animal fats, whisked egg whites, and tree resins like mastic. Flash forward to Europe in the 1800s and the craze for bright appearances was still going strong, with women adorning their hair with gold, silver, or diamond powders.[34]

On the one hand, it might seem anachronistic to suggest that materials such as pyrite or diamond count as "glitter." But when we remember the word's origins as a verb, we remember that glitter comes from nature. The sun, water, ice, dew, minerals, gems, stars, fire, and flowers can all be said to glitter. Remember British poet Robert Southey's description of a local waterfall in 1802: "glittering and frittering . . . And sprinkling and twinkling . . . And gleaming and streaming and steaming and beaming."[35] Or think of "Glitter Mountain" in Arizona, the site of abundant selenite, the crystallized form of gypsum. Scholar Deborah Bird Rose, inspired by the Yolngu Aboriginal term "Bir'yun," meaning "shimmer" or "brilliance," has suggested that "[b]rilliance allows you . . . into the experience of being part of a vibrant and vibrating world."[36] 5-year-old Rory, whom we met in Chapter 3, would certainly agree with this line of thought; he hypothesizes that glitter is made of stars, collected "in a bucket" by people who "put the spacesuits on" and go to the moon, then mix the glitter with food to give it color. From these perspectives, craft and cosmetic glitters are just one small attempt to replicate the shimmer and glimmer found in nature. As are kindred objects such as sequins, which have been inspired by fish scales and bird plumage.[37] And, often, this replication works: one of (plastic) glitter's major commercial uses is in fishing lures.[38]

These deep links to nature can help us make sense of the fact that, according to the *Online Etymology Dictionary*, it wasn't until 1956 that "glitter" began referring to that specific commercial object used for decoration or adornment.[39] The *Oxford English Dictionary* only added that connotation in 1993—though "glitter bomb" recently made it in, after a much shorter timeline.[40] Ecoglitter seeks to return us to those older roots, while employing contemporary processes and responding to current problems. As we see, then, glitter as a phenomenon is always subject to the contingencies of natural resources, economics, technology, labor, social consciousness, and environmental change.

"Blurring Gender Lines through Shine": Queer Ecologies of Glitter

What is perhaps most interesting about ecoglitter brands such as BioGlitz and Projekt Glitter is how they explicitly market their products to LGBTQ+ communities—thus upholding that glitter-queerness link sketched out in Chapter 1, but in explicitly positive ways.[41] BioGlitz has declared that their "mission is to knock down boundaries [and] preconceived notions of normality, and [to] fuel acceptance with a dash of sparkling color," and their promotional materials feature androgynous/genderqueer models and sexually suggestive imagery such as a bedazzled hand holding up a half-peeled banana.[42] Meanwhile, Projekt Glitter's Instagram account features appearances by Berlin-based gender-bending figures such as Aurah Jendafaaq (say it out loud), Morgan Wood (it's funnier if you speak German), and Lana Labia, the latter of whom identifies as "glitter-bearded glitter-headed non binary drag queen."[43]

More than simply linking their products with LGBTQ+ communities, ecoglitter brands often link environmentalism with queerness. For example, BioGlitz's Instagram account playfully describes the brand as "TAKING THE LITTER OUT OF GLITTER, BLURRING GENDER LINES THROUGH SHINE."[44] I therefore propose considering ecoglitter in light of two affiliated environmentalist movements that happen to have queer resonance: the anti-plastics movement and the sustainable/ethical consumption movement.

Perhaps the most visible queer expression of the anti-plastics movement is the "#PlasticFreePride" campaign developed by Out for Sustainability, a US-based LGBTQ+-focused environmental nonprofit known as OUT4S for short. As their Web page argues, "Pride is the most visible showcase of the LGBTQ community. Yet the early spirit has faded, in part from the huge volume of waste incurred at Pride parades and festivals, and other large queer events." An unrelated image posted on Twitter in 2019 by UK resident Tomasz W. Kozlowski bespeaks this reality: plastic bottles, plastic bags, fast food containers, and other waste line the sidewalks and barricaded streets of London's Whitehall, which are empty save for a few bedraggled celebrants sitting or standing curbside.[45] On a facing building, one section of rainbow flag bunting banner sags noticeably—as if acting out the fall from grace that OUT4S narrates: "The green stripe in our flag"—as conceived by Gilbert Baker in 1978—"is for nature. Let's honor that starting now."[46] Interestingly, an earlier version of the flag also contained "a touch of 'glitter,'"

FIGURE 6 Model LaQuan Lewis shimmers in BioGlitz body glitter. Photo by Elena Kulikova. Courtesy of BioGlitz.

as co-creator Lynn Segerblom recalls: "a lamé star stitched to the aqua stripe, silver lamé on one side, gold lamé on the other side."[47]

OUT4S's site offers anti-plastics advice for attendees as well as vendors and organizers—evading the problematic approach in which environmental activism is reduced to individual actions. For the first group, advice includes, "Adapt something fabulous you have already to show your colors instead of buying fast fashion," and "Use your creativity to avoid plastic beads, glitter, balloons, and other toxic garbage items (think instead natural body paint, flowers, reclaimed materials)." For organizers, advice includes, "Put together a strategy to have #PlasticFreePride in 5 years or less," and, "Start with the basics and ban plastic balloons, glitter, beads, bottles, and dinnerware (replace them all with compostable equivalents)."

While responding to such concerns over plastic pollution, ecoglitter also invokes environmental philosopher Kate Soper's concept of "alternative hedonism," a constellation of emotions and insights that includes disenchantment with the pace of Western consumerism, concern with the "social and environmental exploitation" behind it and, conversely, a recognition of the "pleasures gone missing" in such consumerism, from extra free time to less stress to lack of guilt.[48] In Soper's vision, "the new consumption would be restricted in material terms, but [would] not . . . requir[e] us to forego sensual delight."[49] Consider, for example, how EcoStardust's "Pure Range" glitter avoids plastic but therefore offers greater softness; its lack of aluminum means it is not as shiny, but in its place we can enjoy a "pearlescent, translucent effect."[50] (As physicist Jocelyn Read explained it to me, "the lack of aluminum metal in the alternative ecoglitter means that . . . some angles of incoming light get absorbed/scattered instead of undergoing specular reflection.")[51] Similarly, Lush Cosmetics' ethical use of synthetic mica comes with sensory benefits: "synthetic [mica] has very smooth edges," whereas natural mica "feel[s] uncomfortable around the eyes."[52]

Perhaps buying ecoglitter is still too frivolous a pursuit for the world that Soper imagines. But the fact remains that its purveyors harness the emotions and insights of alternative hedonism. For example, Lush promises guilt-free gilt: "Of all the glitter and lustre that flows out through your bathroom, some of which may make its way back to the ocean, it will all be harmless for the environment, and stand against child labour."[53] The slogan of Pura Bioglitter is more direct: "BRILHE SEM CULPA," or, "SHINE WITHOUT GUILT."[54] So, both literally and figuratively, ecoglitter *feels better*. And in their concerns over both labor and biodegradability, these brands at least begin to oppose the status quo in which the "magical qualities of the commodity . . . obliterate [its] origins *and* [its] final destination."[55]

These queer and emotional dimensions of ecoglitter have larger political and philosophical resonance as well. First, despite the environmental consciousness represented in Baker's 1978 Pride flag, the connection between queer and environmental activism has only entered public consciousness recently, thanks to groups such as OUT4S and Queers for the Climate and the rise of the academic subfield known as "queer ecology." Ecoglitter brands, especially as they appear on social media and in magazines, potentially introduce this connection to broader audiences. Or more to the point: ecoglitter literally embodies this connection.

Second, and relatedly, ecoglitter pointedly activates stances such as indulgence, playfulness, joy, and sensual delight for environmentalist ends. As Projekt Glitter describes their founding realization in 2016, "festivity & fun, frivolity & fabulousness need not be harmful to the Earth we call home."[56] While such stances have been central to queer liberation movements—"our pleasure is our resistance," as Jill Dolan puts it[57]—they have historically been missing from environmentalist movements in the Global North, what with their reputation for doom-and-gloom messaging and killjoy personalities. (Perhaps BioGlitz's next slogan should be, "REPLACING DOOM AND GLOOM WITH SHIMMER AND GLIMMER"!) In other words, ecoglitter reminds us that the pleasure politics of queer culture have great relevance to environmentalism.

To be fair, the aforementioned stereotypes of environmentalists have been crafted in large part by anti-environmentalists, and may differ across cultures. And there are plenty of stories about environmentalist festivity and "sensual delight"; members of the German Green Party, for instance, have been known for their song-singing, wine-drinking, flower-carrying, and even a little light cross-dressing.[58] But in any case, it's clear that ecoglitter products attempt to disrupt the classic associations among glitter, queerness, pollution, contagion, toxicity, and unnaturalness, and model (queer) environmentalisms marked by positive feelings and aesthetic appreciation. And their promise of biodegradability means that the playful Lady Gaga quotation referenced in Chapter 1, "Being gay is like glitter; it never goes away," is somewhat moot—or, at least, only part of the story. While being gay might never go away, it seems that glitter, in the right composition and under the right conditions, sometimes can.

Taste Test: Glitter Beer

Scene 1, Product 1

In June 2019, when this book is just a gleam in my eye, I stumble into Tractor Brewing Co. in Albuquerque with my friends Brian, Josette, and Rob, seeking shelter from a dry lightning storm. We sidle up to the long bar in this large hangar-type space. I look up to see "Queer Beer with Glitter" on the menu, with a promise that profits go to Equality New Mexico, a local LGBTQ+ rights organization. I simply *must* have it.

I drink nearly half of this pretty mediocre ale—which merits a 3.59/5 on Untappd, and whose flavor the site describes as "[m]alty sweetness, orange and tangerine with hints of peach"[59]—before I ask the bartender where the glitter is. She tells me to point my cellphone flashlight at the pint glass, and I see it: tiny sparkles swirling in the coppery liquid. Yet again, glitter is dynamic and contingent; dependent on perception. And, of course, I begin to like the beer more. Blogger Jeff Alworth recounts an observation from brewers Madeleine McCarthy and Lee Hedgmon: you "can't just dump glitter into a mediocre beer and expect it to transform the experience . . . And yet visuals *do* transform the experience. It's an object lesson in how much appearance factors into our mental formulation of 'flavor.'"

We never get called up for karaoke at Tractor Brewing Co. despite putting our names in hours earlier—though our bartender does. But we can't complain when a conga line breaks out to Harry Belafonte's "Jump in the Line (Shake, Senora)." Somewhere there is a video of Rob and I snaking ecstatically through the room, beers in hand, cheers-ing and cajoling those still sitting at the bar with their glitter-less beers.

Scene 2, Product 2

It's still June 2019 and I'm back in Southern California, just in time for the first-ever San Pedro Pride Festival. My friends Matt and Shane and I make a beeline to the beer tent, where we find Elysian Brewing's limited-release "GLITTERis Pride Ale." I swear I have not planned this. But we know very well by now how glitter haunts you, and glitter beer seems no different, at least for me.

Elysian's tasting notes describe the cream ale as "tak[ing] the stage with a sparkling base of Premium 2-Row, C-15, and DextraPils malts," while "Mandarina hops star for a fruit-forward character. For extra rainbow flavor, blackberry and raspberry puree were added to the fermenter."[60] Note the euphemisms of "fruit" and "rainbow," and how the description—"taking the stage" and "starring"—queers and animates this drink. But as the *American Craft Beer* blog explains, this is a glitter beer "in name only . . . Turns out the only actual glitter you'll find in GLITTERis Pride Ale is on its label."[61] And yet, if tasteless glitter can inform our sense of a beer's flavor, then surely the *concept* of glitter can as well. In any case, I ultimately find this beer to be tastier than "Queer Beer with Glitter."

Scene 3, Product 3

In which I take matters into my own hands. I purchase, for $9.99 on the Internet, a 5-gram vial of "All Natural Cocktail Glitter in Gold" from Snowy River Cocktails, a company that has an expansive line of cocktail- and beer-decorating products as well as its own brick-and-mortar bars. The ingredients, per the label, are turmeric and "mica-based pearlescent."

I next pay a visit to Trademark Brewing, a local Long Beach brewery, to select the beer I'll bedazzle. The "Star Guide Hazy IPA" beckons in a purple can: "[f]ollow us to some righteous intergalactic haze . . . with oats, wheat and pale malts." This cosmological drink seems well-suited to the otherworldly shimmer of glitter, and I purchase a 4-pack. (I also buy a 4-pack of something called "Cricket Sweater" because, you know, the name.)

The directions on the vial advise me to "lightly mix in a smidgen for a sparkly finish"—a smidgen, they note, being "<0.07% by alcohol weight." My beers are 16 ounces each and I can't do math, so I throw a pinch in a pint glass. It lasts for 2 beers, and then I use what's leftover to add more sparkle to some sparkling water. Yet again, glitter sticks around and keeps on giving—for better or worse!

The beer is sweetly acidic and provides the necessary buzz for the evening's activities: group-chatting online with old grad-school friends as we make our way through *Monkeys, Go Home!*, a forgotten (by most) live-action Disney film from

1967 about an American who inherits a French olive grove and coerces chimpanzees to pick the fruit. (Yes, the film features a Marxist subplot, and, no, I'm not making any of this up.)

The glitter creates great swirly clouds that, appropriate to the "Star Guide" name, resemble a galaxy. It reminds me of a painting I once saw, Lucio Fontana's *Concetto Spaziale* (1957), which mixes oil, sand, and glitter on a perforated canvas to approximate "a transforming cosmic energy . . . of galactic space or a planetary body."[62] The suspension is quite good, which is probably helped by my constant drinking and pouring. As Alworth notes, "What you can't appreciate from still photos is that glitter exposes how dynamic a beer is. The tiny flecks ride the currents in bands and whorls, following the convection of released carbon dioxide or the motion of the drinker's hand. . . . It's riveting."[63] Wish I could say the same for *Monkeys, Go Home!*

You might argue that my DIY method of creating a glitter beer is cheating. But brewers such as Cat Wiest report that they always add glitter at the end of the process because of the suspension issue. She told me that she gave up on bottling or canning glitter beers for this reason; the most common method she employed was "injecting the glitter into the beer while it was being kegged, then storing those kegs upside down until tapping." But "bartenders hate this," she notes, so she "mostly only served the glitter beer at special releases or festivals." Similarly, when explaining why she didn't just dump glitter into the fermentation tank while brewing, McCarthy told Alworth she was worried about it getting into the carbonation stone, or just generally "where it didn't belong." Of course—and this is the point—many would say that beer is precisely where glitter does not belong.

5 CONCLUSION

FACING THE PLASTICENE

All that will remain after an apocalypse is glitter.
—**BRITISH *VOGUE,* as quoted in A.E. Stallings'
poem "Glitter"**[1]

This book opened with a salty takedown of the so-called "Great Glitter Backlash," which has zeroed in on glitter as a microplastic pollutant. But the conditions of this backlash—a growing recognition of the severity of plastic pollution—still deserves further attention, particularly for how it asks us to think of our current era as one with major implications for the coming decades, centuries, and even far beyond. We now pick up that thread; while the rest of this book has offered a (surely idiosyncratic) cultural history of glitter, let's speculate here on glitter's possible futures.

The Age of Plastic

"Can anyone dispute that we live in the Plastic Age when two years of plastic production equals the weight of every man, woman, and child on earth?" Captain Charles Moore, the identifier of the Great Pacific Garbage Patch whom we met in Chapter 1, recently posed this question, noting that this "is the first time in history that the material that defines the age is not reused."[2] Following the naming conventions of planetary periodization—the Pleistocene, the Holocene, etc.—some have proposed the Plasticene for our time. Marine ecologists explain that this name "describes the current period in geological history, beginning in the mid-20th century, with the exponential increase in global production, consumption, and disposal of plastic products."[3]

The Plasticene maps onto the Anthropocene, a concept that has been proposed from within the scientific community. Both terms hold that humans are now leaving their mark on the Earth in unprecedented ways and at unprecedented scales. But the Plasticene highlights something very specific, which is that plastic will be one of humankind's most plentiful and enduring legacies. Indeed, this term emerged from research suggesting "that the vast discarding of plastics will be observable in the fossil record, given that plastic can fuse with rock . . . to create plastiglomerates."[4] In other words, the Plasticene asks us to think of the plastic products we engage with every day, such as the cheap PVC sleds I bought while writing this chapter, as "future fossils."[5] As Moore notes, at the rate things are going, "it might not take a century for plastic to coat the ocean surface."[6]

So while I am wary of the collapse between the categories of "glitter" and "plastic," it might be worth taking a few moments to consider how the former substance can help us grasp and grapple with the Plasticene—and provide a meta-opportunity to think through objects as objects.

We could begin with the idea of "scale effects," put forth by literary scholar Timothy Clark: "at a certain . . . threshold, numerous human actions, insignificant in themselves (heating a house, clearing trees, flying between the continents . . .) come together to form a new, imponderable physical event, altering the basic ecological cycles of the planet."[7] And so perhaps the problem of glitter and its dispersal mimes the strange feeling of being alive in the Plasticene/Anthropocene: the more that individual responsibility is diluted—by more people engaging in that action—the greater the cumulative impact. An individual bit of glitter is both significant and insignificant only in relation to the rest of a batch of glitter. To oversimplify it, what is true of glitter is true of all the other products and actions that contribute to environmental problems: things add up.

The paradoxical dispersibility and stickiness of glitter is similarly evocative. Waste, especially plastic waste, spreads and then sticks around *somewhere*, usually in the geographic regions inhabited by poor people to which it is exported or on whose shores it washes up. More pointedly, as scholars of "waste colonialism" have argued, waste tends to be invisible for the rich and visible for the poor.[8] But glitter is somewhat different. Even when one wishes to be rid of it, it sticks to its immediate points of contact as well as to more extended ones, producing forensic traces, as we saw in Chapter 2. Indeed, stickiness is one of the qualities most bemoaned by glitter haters. Glitter is also typically hyper-visible due to its colorfulness and/or shininess. Perhaps then we could say that it reminds us of how "cast-off [consumer] good[s]" *otherwise* typically fall "prey to . . . a 'conspiracy of blindness.'"[9] Glitter's ostentatious, obstinate failure to fit that formula therefore constitutes what Freud would call the "return of the repressed": it potentially reminds us, for instance, that US citizens cast off an average of 4.4 pounds of unrecycled waste per person every day—though certainly some cast off much more than others.[10]

Approaching the Plasticene

So, it seems clear that we have been barreling toward the Plasticene in a hellish handbasket, if we have not already arrived. How might we respond to this present-future? How might we do so with, or in relation to, glitter? How can we honor the valid concerns behind the Great Glitter Backlash while remaining critical of its problematic implications? What is glitter's place in this era of plastic? Let's take a little jaunt through recent queer and feminist thinking to explore some answers.

Performance theorist Katie Schaag takes a pragmatic approach to such questions, arguing that "[s]tudies of the utopian politics of queer aesthetics must consider the environmental cost of materials like [plastic] glitter and silicone, and studies of plastic's toxic impact on the environment should acknowledge the positive role it has played in destabilizing naturalized gender roles and facilitating new forms of pleasure."[11] In this sense, potential use of materials such as (plastic) glitter would entail some kind of cost-benefit analysis. Is it necessary or not? Worth it or not? Or, better, having recognized the environmental problems, we could look for queer solutions. Perhaps one would find that (plastic) glitter could be replaced by some of the other materials and strategies I discuss further below.

Another, related stance might be to embrace, rather than deny, associations between categories such as queerness, femininity, "waste," and "mess"—those associations that have informed reactions against glitter. In his work on the cramped, cluttered living conditions of LGBTQ+ urban dwellers in Manila and New York City, scholar Martin F. Manalansan IV explains that the idea of "[q]ueer as mess refers to material and affective conditions . . . as well as an analytical stance that resists the 'cleaning up' function of the normative."[12] Relatedly, my colleague Hannah Kate Boast once described to me the experience of hosting feminist club nights at a local practice space in England: she received "regular complaint[s] from the men who ran the space about the amount of glitter left behind"—an ironic complaint, given that the space was otherwise filthy on its own. So a strategy for dealing with the Plasticene, and specifically with how glitter has become implicated in it in homophobic and misogynistic ways, might be to engage in something like "strategic irritation": reveling in acts of queer and female messiness that disturb those in power—including refusing to do the typically-feminized labor of cleaning up.

More nihilistically, in an opinion piece for *Slate* on the Great Glitter Backlash, writer Eleanor Cummins sighed, "yeah, we can go ahead and ban glitter. But no one should be fooled into thinking a war on glitter will really save the oceans. The end of the world seems close. Let it sparkle."[13] Taking a similarly controversial stance, cultural and media theorist Heather Davis has suggested that we consider how plastic ushers in new "queer futures."[14] She highlights plastic's potential to disrupt human hormone functioning and reproductive capacity, its ability to act as a host to new microbial lifeforms in the ocean, and its astonishing volume and durability. These facts suggest that, more than (just) future children or grandchildren, we humans are leaving behind plastic progeny. Davis is fascinated by how this scenario sidesteps normative heterosexual genealogies.

As an object, (plastic) glitter could be said to both capture and facilitate some of the developments Davis describes. And considering how I've described glitter connecting bodies, making new "converts," and producing joyful collectivities, glitter might be the perfect emblem of the scenario she imagines, in which "alternative forms of kinship" replace biological reproduction.[15] On a more pragmatic but still theoretical level, we could also entertain scientists' suggestion that, because of its relative "individuality of composition," (plastic) glitter "has the potential to be an indicator microparticle for ascertaining microplastic sources." Somewhat perversely, then, we might embrace glitter as an "environmentally-valuable microplastic": a symptom that could help us trace the origins of the disease.[16]

But I am not fully satisfied with the above lines of speculation. For one thing, correlating plastic with the future feels somewhat cliché—considering that such correlations have been circulating for roughly a century, back to Leo Baekeland's invention of the first synthetic, mass-produced plastic. (Not to mention, yet again, the fact that plastic glitter makes up a tiny fraction of worldwide plastic pollution.) Associating this substance with the future also accepts plastic's insidious strategy of making itself feel inevitable. And in fact, scholars, scientists, and journalists have often been rather rigid in their thinking about glitter, making supposedly common-sense declarations such as, "[g]litter is a collection of small, reflective plastic fragments," "[glitter is a] material (solid)," and "[g]litter is a petroleum product."[17]

But as I have been hinting, and will outline further below, more creative futures are possible. Any discussion of glitter in the context of the Plasticene—if we care to confront this present-future at all—must focus on expanding our notions of glitter, in ways both material and conceptual. Glitter, so deeply associated with plastic, has at the very least forced us to think about the impacts of that material. But might it even be a tool with which to *quit* plastic?

All That Is Glitter Does Not Necessarily Glitter?

We already heard in Chapter 4 that glitter was historically made from organic materials such as mica and pyrite, and more recently from organic materials such as salt and sugar. But I want to pull back for a moment here and think about the conceptual paths that can continue to help us expand glitter in the future. I suggested earlier that glitter might be an *effect* more than an *object*—or, at least, that effects might be more important than objects or their constitution.[18] That is, people are surely more enamored of what glitter does and what it represents than what it's made out of; its functionality rather than its materiality. As Jeanne Low of Projekt Glitter reports, the alternative festival crowd she serves with her ecoglitters "values experiences over just buying products." Thinking along these lines opens glitter up as an object.[19]

Considering the complex emotional implications of glitter that this book has surveyed, could we also think of glitter not just in terms of *effects* but also *affects*—of feelings? Could we redefine glitter as something that sparks a sense of joy, collectivity, self-assurance, and/or extroversion? If glitter can be a feeling, can it also, building on the last chapter, be a taste? Remember that at least one beverage marketed as a "glitter beer," Elysian's "GlitterIS Pride Ale," contains no such substance at all, just a "fruit-forward character and . . . blackberry meets raspberry flavor."[20] Here, we might also think in the figurative sense of taste. Many would describe flamboyant practices such as covering oneself in glitter or performing in drag as exhibiting campy "taste"—or, as the case may be, "tastelessness."[21]

Maybe glitter is a color? At least one blogger has argued for that conception, pointing out that "a color cannot be described, it cannot have limitations because a color is a figment of our imagination."[22] They made that argument using a purply-pink font I might call "orchid"—but, of course, that's my subjective imagination. Ph.D. student Alexi Garrett told me that she once dressed *as* glitter for Halloween, wearing a silver tube top, silver hot pants, a silver glitter headband, and silver glitter flats, spraying herself in glue and then covering herself in silver glitter. While it would seem that she imagines glitter as silver, perhaps the shiny effect of silver is most important. I can't help but think here of a non sequitur quip from the absurdist comedian Julio Torres, who often performs with glitter on his face and hands: "As you can probably tell by now, my favorite color is clear, followed closely by shiny."[23] I myself have maintained a collection of translucent fashion items over the years, including a bracelet, a belt, and shoes, in addition to shiny and sparkly accessories. So, as you can probably tell by now, my favorite comedian is Julio Torres. *Clearly* (ha) we are both trendsetters pushing the boundaries of common-sense categories. And if you think he has pushed too far, recall from science class that not even pink or black or white are colors by the strict definition of that word.[24]

What I'm suggesting, in a silly way, is that if we focus on what glitter *does*, or on how we *experience it*, perhaps we can then expand our ideas of or expectations for what it *is*. Let's return to Todd Haynes' film *Velvet Goldmine*, which we explored in Chapter 1, for some expansion-inspiration. In an early concert scene, we meet glitter/glam rock star Brian Slade (Jonathan Rhys Myers), a fictionalized amalgamation of real-life stars David Bowie and Jobriath whose name also nods to the band Slade. Brian Slade stalks onstage in a skintight jumpsuit with glittering holographic V-shaped panels and a giant feather collar piece studded with sequins.[25] A quick shot shows us that feathers have been attached to ventilator fans in the concert venue, causing the down to float through the air and onto the enraptured crowd in much the same way as we saw glitter do in the children's film *Spies in Disguise* and the AIDS activism film *120 BPM*. That is to say, the feathers in this scene function as glitter: they float and coat and circulate and disperse and entrance and provide tactile sensations. They create out of mundane space a magical, communal atmosphere.

A sequence near the end of the film makes a similar case for the interchangeability of materials that function as glitter—while also making a metafictional case for glitter as imaginary, in multiple senses. As journalist and former Brian Slade fan Arthur Stuart (Christian Bale) makes love to Curt

Wild (Ewan McGregor) on a rooftop, the first notes of the Cockney Rebel song "Tumbling Down" begin and glitter starts, well, tumbling down from the sky. The shot fades out to black but the glitter is still visible and the song continues; we then fade into a new shot where glitter continues to tumble down and Brian Slade, wearing glittery green face makeup, begins to sing the lyrics to "Tumbling Down" in what appears to be an empty mansion. At one point in the latter scene, Slade scales a chandelier and begins throwing white rose petals from aloft. Visually and affectively, the petals become nearly interchangeable with the falling glitter; like the feathers earlier, they function as an organic glitter analogue. (The title of "Tumbling Down" also provides a punny callback to the falling feathers, though I'm sure I'm overthinking that.)

Here, glitter is again connective and collective, just as music is—tying together the different characters and the different threads of the plot, which skips among past and present, fantasy and reality. (And remember from Chapter 3 that sound is part of how we conceive of glitter, even if unrealistically so.) The Mariah Carey movie *Glitter*, while arguably of different quality than *Velvet Goldmine*, contains flourishes with similar functions: a shot of fireworks and, later, one of glitter, serve as transitions between scenes and time periods. Glitter and its analogues are formally, as well as socially and emotionally, connective.

Much like glitter, both feathers and petals function in nature to communicate with or attract other creatures;

think of male peacocks presenting their plumage to females, or fragrant flowers awaiting their bee pollinators. Nature writer Ellen Meloy's gorgeous ode to desert blooms dramatizes the latter scenario: the "claret cup cactus grows in dense clusters of cylindrical green stems topped by scarlet blossoms so seductive, you want to . . . fall facedown into the lush halo of nectar inside each cup-shaped flower and wallow there."[26] And both objects go beyond what the average person would summarize as glitter's effects—namely, sparkling, shining, decorating, and/or adorning—to include creating community, connection, atmosphere, ecologies.

The fact that the glitter in *Velvet Goldmine* was surely added digitally reminds us of other ways in which contemporary humans engage with glitter: not materially but virtually, as through image filters on social media and photo-processing programs. On Instagram, for example, I can take a picture of myself and enhance it with animated falling sparkles—choice of green, yellow, or rainbow—or animated stars that flicker between white and purple before quickly "bursting": flashing brightly, leaving behind a halo, and disappearing. On the Japanese messaging app Line, one can choose from among 5 different filters: "Sparkle," "Cosmos," "Blue Dust," "Ruby Dust," and "Gold Dust." While the title of this book series, *Object Lessons*, might suggest otherwise, glitter need not be tangible at all, much less plastic, for one to enjoy its effects.

Etymologies of Glitter

As we noted earlier, "glitter" was a verb for approximately 200 years before it was a noun. This move from verb to noun mirrors the material development of glitter. That is, the word shifted from indicating an effect to indicating an object—and, more specifically and recently, a commodity. The same, interestingly, is true for plastic: "[u]ntil the invention of the material itself that goes by that name, the word *plastic* was never a noun, but an adjective . . . a *quality* defined by its capacity to be formed and transformed."[27] (Ironically, of course, plastic doesn't transform *enough*, insofar as it does not effectively biodegrade.) Inspired by the plasticity of the word itself—shifting from verb to noun, and from noun to adjective, as we'll see below—I propose a new plasticity to the understanding of what is and can be glitter. That is, I propose that we take up the notion of *glitter as plastic*, but in that original sense of "flexible," not "made of synthetic polymers"—as we have seen so many people assume.

When it comes to the noun, we have just seen how materials such as feathers and petals, in addition to pyrite, mica, salt, sugar, cellulose, etc., could conceptually fit under its sign. Perhaps, inspired by the recipes circulated by the Mexican protestors we met in Chapter 2, we could also imagine glitter not as a market commodity but as something homemade and traded—which would mean a move back toward the earlier version of the noun form, if not the verb form.

Meanwhile, the verb form might expand beyond the literal effects of sparkling, shining, or drawing attention, to include ideas such as "producing collectives," "marking celebration," or "provoking joy." After all, as philosopher Thomas Leddy muses, something might "sparkle metaphorically if it produces effects in us similar to that of literal sparkle . . . Metaphorical sparkle and shine point to deeper dimensions of experience."[28] Simply put, to say that something "glitters" might mean more than just, "it *literally* sparkles."

I am reminded here of "Gay Wedding Advice," a 2014 sketch from the Comedy Central show *Key & Peele*. The sketch features a gay African-American man (Keegan-Michael Key) who is subjected to ridiculous questions from his coworker's African-American family members, who are perturbed about what to expect at their cousin's upcoming same-sex wedding. "Do we throw something other than rice?" asks one family member (Romany Malco). "Like what, sir? What would you throw other than rice?!" demands the exasperated man. "I dunno. I dunno," the family member responds. "Couscous. Skittles." Clearly intended as a joke about perceptions of difference, this punchline offers the same general proposition that I do: that we could retain the effects of certain objects— their emotional and taste-related implications and functions— while playing fast and loose with their composition.

Of course, countless objects have changed their composition over time. As a child, to take one memorable example, I was both fascinated and repulsed by the horse-hair bristles of my great-aunt's wooden-handled hairbrush;

most hairbrushes had become entirely plastic before I was born. And language constantly evolves. Glitter is not unique or unusual in those senses. But I have particular confidence in its possibilities of change because glitter moves in so many other ways. It moves conceptually between various poles, depending on the viewpoints involved—between frivolous and functional, pointless and political, dangerous and harmless, visible and inscrutable, vengeful and playful, anxiety-producing and pleasure-inducing. In these senses, it moves people *emotionally*—whether toward love or hate or both at the same time.

Further, as we have previously seen, glitter is flexible enough to, in the cultural imagination, stand in for everything from homosexuality to immigrants to coronavirus. And both the verb and the noun form entail dynamism, relay, movement. Deborah Bird Rose puts the phenomenon beautifully, riffing on the experience of light on water: "It is a capture that is all over the place: water capturing and reflecting the sun, the sun glinting on the water, the eyes of the beholders captured and enraptured, the ephemeral dance of it all. It is equally a lure: creatures long to be grabbed, to experience that beauty, that surprise, that gleaming ephemeral moment of capture."[29]

Recalling the earlier point about adjectives, we might also note that "glitter" serves the latter role in some formulations. Consider the many articles that trumpeted the recent discovery of so-called "glitter worms," whose "iridescent scales look like costume sequins."[30] "Glitter worms," rather than "glitter*y* worms" or "glitter*ing* worms," suggests that the creatures are made of this substance, or decorated with it. Of course, that's not the case, oceanic microplastic pollution notwithstanding: these worms naturally emit color and shine. But scientific accuracy is less the point here than the fact that "glitter" signifies celebration, relief, and wonder to many people. Indeed, when much of the world was entering Covid-19 lockdown in May 2020, comedian and journalist Bonnie Burton somewhat inaccurately but enthusiastically Tweeted: "Listen: the world is kinda rough right now. But scientists just discovered a GLITTER-COVERED WORM at the bottom of the ocean and we need to talk about it!"[31]

Burton shares a similar outlook with Australian/US art duo Pony Express, who recently announced that they want to present "'palliative strategies'" to make "our apocalypse 'more mutual, comfortable, maybe even pleasurable.'"[32] Their art installation *Ecosexual Bathhouse*, for instance, allows participants to pop on a finger condom and hand-pollinate various orchid species. Pony Express would seem to agree with Eleanor Cummins that the end of the world is actually the *most*, not least, appropriate time to reach for frivolous objects and practices, but their case for doing so centers pointedly on values of collective care. They call for everyone to find pleasure and beauty together, in the moment, without requiring naïve optimism or false hopes for the future. So, whereas this chapter's epigraph locates glitter *after* the apocalypse—presumably because of its frequent lack of biodegradability and its stubborn persistence in terms of dispersibility and stickiness—perhaps glitter is a tool with which we can *face* it, together.

We could also take this chapter's epigraph in a slightly different sense than perhaps it was intended: as suggesting that the human need to decorate, to celebrate, and to behold beauty—for and with others—has persisted throughout time and will continue to do so. There will always be desire for glitter, whether by that we mean the sparkle and shine of natural elements, the commodity used in crafts and cosmetics, or a broadened category like the one I sketched out above: small aggregate objects or visual effects that tumble, spill, or circulate, creating sensuous communal atmospheres.

We might also remember that "[a]pocalypse does not equal annihilation: etymologically it means revelation," that of a new world to come.[33] The compositional and conceptual changes I've described mark the flexibility of "glitter" as a category. Glitter has always been a matter of fantasy and fabulosity, so why not imagine more for it and more *of* it? But more broadly, those changes might mark a promising turn toward adaptation, even toward a post-Plasticene world-to-come. Even despite consumer-capitalist limitations, perhaps we humans can remake what we mean by so many object designations. Or, at least, find pleasure in trying.

ACKNOWLEDGMENTS

This book was made possible by an Alumni Fellowship at the Rachel Carson Center for Environment and Society (RCC), an Environmental Humanities Visiting Research Fellowship at the Institute for Advanced Studies in the Humanities (IASH) at the University of Edinburgh, and a semester-long sabbatical from California State University, Fullerton. The Wirzbicki Fund for Student-Faculty Research, endowed at Fullerton's English Department, also generously allowed Gabe Taggard and Johnny Weil to provide research assistance.

The fellows and visiting scholars of the RCC were particularly helpful in providing feedback and conviviality, and particularly destructive in providing Glühwein and Țuică. Thank you to Antoine Acker, Anna Antonova, Johanna Conterio, Rowan Deer—whose knack for etymology proved invaluable—Alfonso Donoso, Stefan Dorondel, Stephen Halsey, Ute Hasenhörl, Cherry Leonardi, Julia Leyda, Anna Mazanik, Steve Milder, Roger Norum, Huiying Ng, Milica Prokic—with whom I re-experienced *Velvet Goldmine* and, therefore, my youth, alongside Ross Maidment—Kate Rigby,

Alessandro Rippa, William San Martín, Danielle Schiel, Astrid Schrader, Tom Smith, Sevgi Mutlu Sirakova, and Tracie Wilson. Arielle Helmick and Katie Ritson are, as always, my favorite Munich ambassadors. Lena Engel, Charlotte Huber, Laura Mann, and many other staff members and student assistants made things functional and fun. Thank you also to Christof Mauch and Helmuth Trischler for creating a world-renowned center that has changed so many lives.

Ben Fletcher-Watson at IASH got the ball rolling on the "Glitter Bar" event for the Edinburgh Science Festival that this book happily showcases. Shy Zvouloun and, of course, my co-hostess with the mostest, Mystika Glamoor, were also central in pulling it off. Thank you to all our plucky participants! Thank you also to Michelle Bastian, Alexandra Coțofană, Marit Fält, Zsuzsanna Végh, David Farrier, Jarita Holbrook, Anna Pilz, Cristina Richie, Frances Ulman, Jivitesh Vashisht, Rona Wilkie, and Annabel Williams for showing me a good time in Edinburgh. (Hiya, as they say there!)

Rebecca Coleman is, I believe, the first academic to write a book on glitter, and she generously shared her galleys with me early on. If you haven't already, read the wonderful *Glitterworlds: The Future Politics of a Ubiquitous Thing* (2020, Goldsmiths Press).

Many, many other people have written about glitter, especially on blogs and in online articles, and it would be impossible to acknowledge them all here or in the book. But their enthusiasm was infectious and galvanizing for me.

The following people were particularly helpful and generous, whether by suggesting references, making introductions, agreeing to be interviewed, providing encouragement, or setting off some other kind of spark: Parisa Ahmadi, Jeff Alworth, Chris Barton, J Blackwell, Hannah Kate Boast, Lydia Bottegoni, Amanda Boetzkes, Max Bruce, Jill Burke, Alexandra Campbell, CAConrad, Louise Creechan, Vanbasten Noronha de Araújo, Josh Epstein, Jacob J. Erickson, Alexi Garrett, Dannielle Senga Green, Hillary of The Makeup Museum, Reed Hutchinson, John Jarboe, Taylor Mac, Sherilyn MacGregor, Machine Dazzle, Molly Mapstone, Salma Monani, Derek Mong, Leonie Müller, Gabriela Nuñez, Jenny Price, Jocelyn Read, Matt Ruccio, Jade Sasser, Patricia Schneider-Zioga, Maria Sledmere, Christy Tidwell, Emma Train, Marianna Szczygielska, Sarah Wald, Sara Warner, Sarah Pierce Waters, Cat Wiest, Bethany Wiggan, and Youxi Woo. Thank you also to all the organizers and participants at the Mellon Summer Institute in the Environmental Humanities at Colby College, especially Stephanie Bernhard, who helped me turn this book proposal into a successful sabbatical application.

Throughout the writing of this book, I gave several talks to enthusiastic audiences who offered brilliant feedback— especially the students of Katharina Gerstenberger's class at the University of Utah (including Gardiner Allen, Amber Aumiller, Madeleine Bavley, Sam Nelson, and Doug Sam), and those who tuned into talks at Cornell University, Frei Universität Berlin, Swarthmore College, UC Riverside, UC

Santa Barbara, Universidad de Alcalá, Universität Augsburg, University College Dublin, and the University of Edinburgh. I also want to thank all the organizers of those events for their efforts and enthusiasm.

At home in California, many friends provided camaraderie as I wrote this book, including Ella Ben Hagai, Darin DeWitt, Rickey Goodling (you haven't lived until a friend writes an entire trivia round on glitter in your honor!), Lily House-Peters, Kelly Sharron, and Abe Weil. Hugs, my buds.

Monika Christodoulou, Molly Nilsson, Angel Olsen, and T. Rex provided the imagetrack and soundtrack for *Glitter*. Adrian Frutiger designed the Avenir typeface in which I originally composed it. ("Avenir," fittingly for a book on a substance that often feels space-age-y, means "future" in French.)

If I have forgotten to acknowledge or cite anyone, I apologize for the oversight and send you a shimmery embrace in recompense!

BIOGRAPHY

Nicole Seymour is Associate Professor of English and Graduate Advisor for Environmental Studies at California State University, Fullerton. She has written on topics ranging from vegan satire to feminist plastic art to digital drag shows. She is the author of *Bad Environmentalism: Irony and Irreverence in the Ecological Age* (2018).

NOTES

Diary Entry

1 "How Teachers Can Talk to Children about Coronavirus Disease (COVID-19)," UNICEF, https://www.unicef.org/georgia/how -teachers-can-talk-children-about-coronavirus-disease-covid-19.

2 Ken McGrath (@DrKenMcGrath), "Have you ever come into contact with glitter? Like hugged or shaken hands with someone who was wearing or using it? And for the next two weeks, it hangs around forever and ends up on surfaces you can't recall touching, even after showering & washing? Think of COVID-19 as glitter," Tweet, March 22, 2020, https://twitter .com /DrKenMcGrath /status /1241958161675767808.

3 Dimitri Martin, *These Are Jokes* (New York: Comedy Central Records, 2006), CD/DVD.

Chapter 1

1 Daniel C. Remein, "Decorate," in *Veer Ecology: A Companion for Environmental Thinking*, ed. Jeffrey Jerome Cohen and Lowell Duckert (Minneapolis: University of Minnesota Press, 2017), 90.

2 Capt. Charles Moore with Cassandra Phillips, *Plastic Ocean: How a Sea Captain's Chance Discovery Launched a Determined Quest to Save the Oceans* (New York: Avery, 2011), 307. Microplastics also affect freshwater—including rivers and lakes—but most research to date focuses on oceans.

3 One theory is that "microplastics can reduce reproductive output and fitness in marine species by altering their food consumption and energy allocation," according to Tamara S. Galloway and Ceri N. Lewis, "Marine Microplastics Spell Big Problems for Future Generations," *PNAS* 113, no. 9 (May 5, 2015): 2331. However, scientist Richard Thompson told science writer Alla Katsnelson that the "jury's still out" when it comes to definitively proving that microplastics are harmful long-term to either human or nonhuman populations. Katsnelson, "Microplastics Present Pollution Puzzle," *PNAS* 112, no. 18 (March 1, 2016): 5547. See also https://setac.onlinelibrary .wiley.com/doi/full/10.1002/ieam.1913 and https://www.cell .com/current-biology/pdf/S0960-9822(17)30076-3.pdf on the inconclusiveness of current research.

4 Josh Gabbatiss, "Glitter Should Be Banned Over Environmental Impact, Scientists Warn," *Independent*, November 16, 2017, https://www.independent.co.uk/ environment/glitter-ban-environment-microbead-impact -microplastics-scientists-warning-deep-ocean-a8056196.html.

5 AJ Willingham, "Glitter Is Not Just Annoying, It Could Be Bad for the Environment," *CNN*, November 29, 2017, https:// edition.cnn.com/2017/11/29/health/glitter-environment -hazard-microbead-ban-trnd/index.html. Kate Sheridan, "Glitter Is an Environmental Scourge That is Wrecking the Oceans. Should It Be Banned?", *Newsweek*, November 29, 2017, https://www.newsweek.com/glitter-environmental -scourge-wrecking-oceans-should-it-be-banned-725826.

6 Jacqueline Antonovich, "Glitter is a microplastic . . .", Tweet, December 22, 2018.

7 Adrienne Matei, "Glitter is an Environmental Abomination. It's Time to Stop Using It," *The Guardian*, October 22, 2020, https://www.theguardian.com/commentisfree/2020/oct/22/glitter-environment-microplastics-hazard.

8 Dannielle Senga Green et al., "All That Glitters is Litter? Ecological Impacts of a Conventional Versus Biodegradable Glitter in a Freshwater Habitat," *Journal of Hazardous Materials* 402 (2021): 1.

9 "Biodegradable Glitter Backed by Sir David Attenborough," *BBC*, April 2, 2019, https://www.bbc.com/news/av/uk-england-manchester-47789342 (video). Scientist Richard Thompson told *National Geographic*, "while there is evidence of accumulation of microplastics in general and evidence of harm from lab studies, there is a lack of clear evidence specifically on glitter . . . We have microplastic particles in around one third of the 500 fish we examined in the English Channel, but we did not find any glitter." Laura Parker, "To Save the Oceans, Should You Give Up Glitter?", *National Geographic* November 30, 2017, https://www.nationalgeographic.com/news/2017/11/glitter-plastics-ocean-pollution-environment-spd/.

10 Adam Minter, "Banning Glitter Won't Save the Oceans," *Bloomberg*, October 24, 2020, https://www.bloomberg.com/opinion/articles/2020-10-24/banning-glitter-won-t-save-the-oceans?sref=2o0rZsF1&utm_content=view&cmpid%3D=socialflow-twitter-view&utm_source=twitter&utm_campaign=socialflow-organic&utm_medium=social.

11 Seth Garben, "Who Invented Glitter and Why?" *Guff* 2014, https://guff.com/who-invented-glitter-and-why.

12 Paul Morrison, "Polyester," in *Life in Plastic: Artistic Responses to Petromodernity*, ed. Caren Irr (Minneapolis: University of Minnesota Press, 2021), 37.

13 Chloe Street, "61 UK Festivals Are Banning Glitter," *Evening Standard*, August 6, 2018, https://www.standard.co.uk/beauty/ music-festivals-ban-glitter-microbeads-microplastic-a3812661 .html. Further confusing the issue, plastic was not in fact "outlawed," but self-policed through the initiative, which was developed by the Association of Independent Festivals.

14 Stacy Liberatore, "Scientists Call for a Complete Ban on GLITTER Because the Particles Are Polluting Oceans and Hurting Marine Life," *The Daily Mail*, December 19, 2019, https://www.dailymail.co.uk/sciencetech/article-7777837/ Scientists-call-complete-ban-GLITTER-particles-polluting -oceans.html. PETRA (PET Resin Association), "An Introduction to PET," *Petrisin.org* 2015, http://www.petresin.org /news_introtoPET.asp#:~:text=PET%20(also%20abbreviated%2 0PETE)%20is,soft%20drinks%2C%20juices%20and%20water.

15 Tom Espiner, "Morrisons and Waitrose Ditch Glitter for Christmas," *BBC*, October 14, 2020, https://www.bbc.com/ news/business-54545428.

16 Fiona Harvey, "Nurseries Ban Glitter in Pre-Christmas Drive for Cleaner Seas," *The Guardian*, November 17, 2017, https:// www.theguardian.com/environment/2017/nov/17/nurseries -ban-glitter-in-pre-christmas-drive-for-cleaner-seas.

17 Rebecca Smithers, "Waitrose to Ban Glitter from Own-Brand Products by 2020," *The Guardian*, December 14, 2018, https:// www.theguardian.com/business/2018/dec/14/waitrose-ban -glitter-own-brand-products-2020.

18 See https://www.sunshineglitter.com/ and https://theglitterc offincompany.co.uk/.

19 Penny Whitehouse, "DIY Biodegradable Glitter for Kids," *MotherNatured*, https://mothernatured.com/nature-crafts/diy-biodegradable-glitter/.

20 Katie Schaag, "The Pleasures of Teaching Plastic," *Edge Effects*, October 12, 2019, https://edgeeffects.net/teaching-plastic/.

21 Bella Cacciatore, "The Best Glitter Makeup, According to Drag Artists," *Glamour*, June 26, 2020 https://www.glamour.com/story/best-glitter-makeup.

22 Richard Corson, *Fashions in Makeup from Ancient to Modern Times* (London: Peter Owen, 1972), 572.

23 Julia Leyda, "Playing with Dolls: Girls, Fans, and the Queer Feminism of *Velvet Goldmine*," *Reframing Todd Haynes: Feminism's Indelible Mark*, ed. Theresa Geller and Julia Leyda (Durham: Duke University Press, 2022), 54.

24 David Bowie, "Rebel Rebel," *Diamond Dogs* (New York: RCA Records), 1974.

25 Madison Mason, "Lecturer Examines Gender in College and Everyday Life," *Iowa State Daily*, October 9, 2019, https://www.iowastatedaily.com/news/iowa-state-memorial-union-great-hall-lecture-series-transgender-lgbtqia-history-month-community-college-campus-gender-identity-z-nicolazzo/article_573d8d5a-e9ea-11e9-b2cd-f7b88019db99.html.

26 Dapper Day, "Would you believe Chinese moths and Louis XVI . . ." *Facebook* October 19, 2020, https://www.facebook.com/DapperDay/posts/would-you-believe-chinese-moths-and-louis-xvi-had-a-big-effect-on-native-america/4672929352747687/.

27 "Glitter Hate is Homophobia," *IntoMore*, October 16, 2017, https://www.intomore.com/you/glitter-hate-is-homophobia#!.

28 See https://en.wikipedia.org/wiki/Candide_(operetta) #"Glitter_and_Be_Gay.

29 "Limericks," *NPR.org*, December 2, 2017, https://www.npr.org /2017/12/02/567914080/limericks.

30 Devon Abelman, "Meet Quil Lemons, the 20-Year-Old Using Glitter to Counter Hypermasculinity in His Community," *Allure*, October 4, 2017, https://www.allure.com/story/quil -lemons-glitterboy-makeup-hypermasculinity.

31 Krista Thompson, *Shine: The Visual Economy of Light in African Diasporic Aesthetic Practice* (Durham: Duke University Press, 2015), 21. Thompson details "light-skin bias in color-film stock emulsions . . . and in . . . digital-camera technologies" (22). See also Nadia Latif, "It's Lit! How Film Finally Learned to Light Black Skin," *The Guardian* September 21, 2017, https://www.theguardian.com/film/2017/sep/21/its -lit-how-film-finally-learned-how-to-light-black-skin.

32 See "Glitter Colour Effects and The Bioglitter Equivalents," *Bioglitter.com*, November 5, 2020, https://www .discoverbioglitter.com/bioglitter_physics_of_light/#:~:text =Opalescent%20and%20Iridescent%20glitters%20utilise,spun %20back%20on%20itself%20back.

33 "Sadie Barnette: The New Eagle Creek Saloon," *The Lab*, https://www.thelab.org/projects/2019/5/11/sadie-barnette-the -new-eagle-creek-saloon.

34 Sadie Barnette, "Projects," https://www.sadiebarnette.com/ projects/.

35 Eddy Francisco Alvarez Jr., "Finding Sequins in the Rubble: Stitching Together an Archive of Trans Latina Los Angeles," *TSQ: Transgender Studies Quarterly* 3, no. 3-4 (2016): 622, quoting fashion historian Elizabeth Wilson.

36 See https://www.instagram.com/trashyclothing/?hl=en.

37 Aya El Sharkawy, email correspondence with the author, March 9, 2021.

38 Aya El Sharkawy, "Another Camp or the Second Testament on Camp," *Kohl: A Journal for Body and Gender Research* 6, no. 3 (2020), https://kohljournal.press/another-camp.

39 See also Rebecca Coleman, *Glitterworlds: The Future Politics of a Ubiquitous Thing* (London: Goldsmiths Press, 2020), 5.

40 See Shayda Kafai, "Re-Coding Blood: Menstruation as Activism," *The STEAM Journal* 2, no. 2 (2016), https://scholarship.claremont.edu/cgi/viewcontent.cgi?article=1123&context=steam#:~:text=Rooted%20in%20her%20book%2C%20Power,1) and also Mohammed Rafi Arefin, "Abjection: A Definition for Discard Studies," *Discard Studies*, February 27, 2015, https://discardstudies.com/2015/02/27/abjection-a-definition-for-discard-studies/.

41 Vanbasten Noronha de Araújo, "Shimmery Waste: A Queer Critique of the Narratives on Glitter Pollution," master's thesis, Central European University, 2019, 82. de Araújo and I come to many of the same conclusions around the glitter/queerness connection.

42 Robert Azzarello, *Queer Environmentality: Ecology, Evolution, and Sexuality in American Literature* (New York: Routledge, 2012), 125.

43 A.E. Stallings, "Glitter," *LIKE* (New York: Farrar, Straus, & Giroux, 2018), 49.

44 Remein, "Decorate," 92.

45 Queer theorist Eve K. Sedgwick coined this term to describe fear of effeminacy.

46 Tiffany Do, "Trash Tiki Takes the Food Waste Conversation behind the Bar," *Food Republic*, August 21, 2017, https://www.foodrepublic.com/2017/08/21/trash-tiki-kill-sustainability/.

47 Joe Coburn, "IamA Glitter Manufacturer AMA!" *Reddit* May 27, 2009, https://www.reddit.com/r/IAmA/comments/1nppaa/iama_glitter_manufacturer_ama/.

48 Mary Celeste Kearney, "Sparkle: Luminosity and Post-Girl Power Media," *Continuum: Journal of Media & Cultural Studies* 29, no. 2 (2015): 263.

49 See Craig Martin, *Shipping Container* (London: Bloomsbury Academic, 2016).

Glitter Bar

1 Senga Green et al., "All That Glitters is Litter?", 2.

2 "BioGlitter Pure," *EcoStardust.com*, https://ecostardust.com/collections/ecostardust-biodegradable-glitter-pure.

3 "ECO GLITTER, how is it made?" *Age of Plastic* podcast, March 2019, https://open.spotify.com/episode/2M6FQE3OXN5ttXsk8oyYrl.

Chapter 2

1 Two homicides are described in Bob Blackledge, "GLITTER as Forensic Evidence," August 2007, https://projects.nfstc.org/trace/docs/final/Blackledge_Glitter.pdf. A third is described on a November 2019 episode of the podcast *Endless Thread*, https://www.wbur.org/endlessthread/2019/11/15/glitter-forensic-science.

2 Blackledge, "GLITTER as Forensic Evidence," 13.

3 Rebecca Coleman, "Glitter: A Methodology of Following the Material," *Mai: Feminism & Visual Culture*, May 15, 2019,

https://maifeminism.com/glitter-a-methodology-of-following
-the-material/.

4 L.M. Bogad, *Tactical Performance: Serious Play and Social Movements* (New York: Routledge, 2016), 40, drawing on Tarrow.

5 Jorge Volpi, "Revolución Diamantina," *Reforma*, August 24, 2019, https://www.reforma.com/libre/acceso/accesofb.htm ?urlredirect=/revolucion-diamantina-2019-08-24/op163028.

6 Aguirre, Ixchel, "La diamantina no se borrará," *Luchadoras*, August 20, 2019, https://luchadoras.mx/la-diamantina-no-se -borrara/.

7 de Araújo, "Shimmery Waste," 29.

8 Parity, "Glitter + Ash Wednesday," https://parity.nyc/glitter -ash-wednesday2020.

9 Anya Galli, "How Glitterbombing Lost Its Sparkle: The Emergence and Decline of a Novel Social Movement Tactic," *Mobilization: An International Quarterly* 21, no. 3 (2016): 268.

10 Glitter Hate is Homophobia," *IntoMore* October 16, 2017, https://www.intomore.com/you/glitter-hate-is-homophobia#!.

11 Sam Eifling, "Science Explains Why Glitter Sticks to Everything," *Popular Mechanics*, May 16, 2016, https://www .popularmechanics.com/technology/a20889/science-of-glitters -ability-to-cling-to-everything/. See also Lori Byrd-McDevitt, "Why Does Glitter Stick to Everything?" https://www .childrensmuseum.org/blog/why-does-glitter-stick-everything.

12 Nick Espinosa quoted in NPR Staff, "Glitter-Bombing: A Sparkly Weapon of Disapproval on the Campaign Trail," *NPR.org*, February 16, 2012, https://www.npr.org/sections/itsallpolitics /2012/02/16/147003278/glitter-bombing-a-sparkly-weapon-of -disapproval-on-the-campaign-trail?t=1606665154600.

13 Amory Starr, "Directions for the Anti-Corporate
    Globalization Movement," April 14, 2002, https://amorystarr
    .com/directions-for-the-anti-corporate-globalization
    -movement/.

14 Sam Hind, "Maps, Kettles, and Inflatable Cobblestones,"
    Media Fields Journal: Critical Explorations in Media and Space,
    Friday, August 21, 2015, http://mediafieldsjournal.org/tactical
    -frivolity-and-disobed/#3.

15 Harry Josephine Giles, "Being Fabulously Antifascist:
    Report and Thoughts on Scotland's 'Glitter against
    Fascism,'" *Medium*, August 1, 2016, https://medium.com/@
    harryjosiegiles/being-fabulously-antifascist-report-and-thou
    ghts-on-scotlands-glitter-against-fascism-ac709344debc.

16 Bogad, *Tactical Performance*, 89.

17 Galli, "How Glitterbombing Lost Its Sparkle," 269-270.

18 Andrew Boyd and Joshua Kahn Russell, "Principle: Put Your
    Target in a Decision Dilemma," *Beautiful Trouble: A Toolbox
    for Revolution*, https://beautifultrouble.org/principle/put-your
    -target-in-a-decision-dilemma/.

19 Cowan, "GLITTERfesto," 17.

20 Galli, "How Glitterbombing Lost Its Sparkle," 269-70.

21 Will Potter, "Two Environmentalists Were Charged with
    'Terrorism Hoax' for Too Much Glitter on Their Banner," *Vice*,
    December 18, 2013, https://www.vice.com/amp/en_au/article
    /xd5dxa/two-environmentalists-were-charged-with-terrorism
    -hoax-for-too-much-glitter-on-their-banner. Three years
    later, Stephenson and Warner were acquitted. See http://www
    .okenergytoday.com/2016/08/20336/.

22 Tom Phillips, "Mexico's 'Glitter Revolution' Targets Violence against Women," *The Guardian*, August 26, 2019, https://www.theguardian.com/world/2019/aug/26/desperation-and-rage-mexican-women-take-to-streets-to-protest-unabated-sexual-violence-glitter-revolution.

23 Rebecca Coleman, *Glitterworlds: The Future Politics of a Ubiquitous Thing* (London: Goldsmiths Press, 2020), 142.

24 Nick Duffy, "Queer Dance Troupe Shut Down Traffic at Climate Change Protest by Twerking in Amazing Viral Video," *Pink News*, September 24, 2019, https://www.pinknews.co.uk/2019/09/24/twerking-climate-change-protest-werk-for-peace-washington-dc/.

25 John Jarboe, "The Beards are switching to Eco-Glitter . . .," *Facebook*, December 18, 2018, https://www.facebook.com/john.jarboe.16/posts/10110946215942323. And John Jarboe, "SO excited about this . . .," *Facebook*, January 8, 2019, https://www.facebook.com/john.jarboe.16/posts/10111031318081953.

26 Meg Perret, "Chemical Castration: White Genocide and Male Extinction in Rhetoric of Endocrine Disruption," *NiCHE*, June 9, 2020, https://niche-canada.org/2020/06/09/chemical-castration-white-genocide-and-male-extinction-in-rhetoric-of-endocrine-disruption/. See also Hannah Kate Boast's work on this topic.

27 Jeanne Low, Zoom correspondence with the author, September 30, 2020.

28 Katie Moussouris, "No. Glitter, like so many things, requires enthusiastic, continuous CONSENT," Tweet, January 27, 2019, https://twitter.com/k8em0/status/1089705872111022080.

29 Elahe Izadi, "ShipYourEnemiesGlitter.com Is Already for Sale. 'I'm Sick of Dealing with It,' Site's Founder Says," *Washington Post*, January 16, 2015, https://www.washingtonpost.com/news /morning-mix/wp/2015/01/15/shipyourenemiesglitter-com -founder-please-stop-buying-this-horrible-glitter-product/.

30 Lucy Bacon, "Desk of Gay UCL Officer Glitter Bombed after SU Party in 'Homophobic Attack,'" *The UCL Tab*, https:// thetab.com/uk/london/2018/03/15/desk-of-gay-ucl-officer -glitter-bombed-after-su-party-in-homophobic-attack-31606.

31 Galli, "How Glitterbombing Lost Its Sparkle," 269, drawing on Soule and Tarrow.

32 Carly Rodgers, "The Paradox of Carnaval: Afro-Brazilian Contributions to a National Celebration," *Think Brazil*, February 27, 2018, https://www.wilsoncenter.org/blog-post /the-paradox-carnaval-afro-brazilian-contributions-to -national-celebration.

33 Dom Phillips, "Brazil Carnival Revellers Warned That All That Glitters is Not Good for the Planet," *The Guardian*, February 11, 2018, https://www.theguardian.com/world/2018 /feb/11/brazil-carnival-rio-glitter-microplastics-environment.

34 Rosalind Jana, "Glitter: Through Magnum Images," Magnum Photos, January 22, 2021, https://www.magnumphotos.com/ arts-culture/fashion/glitter-through-magnum-images/.

35 Michele White, "Never Cleaning Up: Cosmetic Femininity and the Remains of Glitter," *Producing Women: The Internet, Traditional Femininity, Queerness, and Creativity* (New York: Routledge, 2015), 162. Earlier variations of this aphorism date back to the 12th century. See https://www.phrases.org.uk/ meanings/all-that-glitters-is-not-gold.html#:~:text=The%20p roverbial%20saying%20'All%20that,and%20superficially%20 attractive%20is%20valuable.

36 Moore with Phillips, *Plastic Ocean*, 40.

37 Jillian Hernandez, *Aesthetics of Excess: The Art and Politics of Black and Latina Embodiment* (Durham: Duke University Press, 2020), 9.

38 Rosalind Galt, *Pretty: Film and the Decorative Image* (New York: Columbia University Press, 2011), 66.

39 Thompson, *Shine*, 25.

40 Of course, these associations don't work the same way in every context. Doug Sam, a University of Utah student, pointed out to me that Chinese people exchange red envelopes encrusted with glitter for Chinese New Year, representing the stimulation of wealth. Here, the glitter is not meant to be tacky or cheap; it is a tangible metaphor for real wealth.

41 Bogard, *Tactical Performance*, 37.

42 While Spring 2011-Spring 2012 was certainly the heyday of glitterbombing, a few random bombings have since cropped up in the United States, such as that of neo-Nazi figurehead Richard Spencer in 2017. For a good time, see https://www.youtube.com/watch?v=fkQ7sDJHHq8.

Poetry Reading

1 Andrew Ridker, "Queer Bubbles," *The Paris Review*, July 6, 2017, https://www.theparisreview.org/blog/2017/07/06/queer-bubbles/.

2 "ECODEVIANCE," Wave Books, https://www.wavepoetry.com/products/ecodeviance.

3 CAConrad, "Glitter in My Wounds," *Poetry*, November 2018, https://www.poetryfoundation.org/poetrymagazine/poems/148106/glitter-in-my-wounds.

4 CAConrad, "The Queer Voice: Reparative Poetry Rituals & Glitter Perversions," *Poetry*, June 22, 2015, https://www.poetryfoundation.org/harriet-books/2015/06/the-queer-voice-reparative-poetry-rituals-glitter-perversions.

5 CAConrad, *ECODEVIANCE: (Soma)tics for the Future Wilderness* (Seattle: Wave Books, 2014), 137.

6 Despite the similarity of meaning, in none of these cases does "gl-" itself operate as a separable unit of meeting, the way that "un-" or "de-" could be added or subtracted to words such as "dress" or "couple." This is an unusual linguistic case known as a "phonestheme."

7 CAConrad, *While Standing in Line for Death* (Seattle: Wave Books, 2017), 36.

8 Emma Train, "CAConrad's Queer Futurities," paper presented at the Association for the Study of Literature andEnvironment Biennial Conference, UC Davis, June 28, 2019, 3.

9 Maria Sledmere, *The Luna Erratum* (Manchester: Dostoyevsky Wannabe Originals, 2021), 94.

Chapter 3

1 Youxi Woo, Zoom interview with the author, June 22, 2021.

2 Thomas Leddy, "Sparkle and Shine," *The British Journal of Aesthetics* 37, no. 3 (July 1997): 269, https://doi.org/10.1093/bjaesthetics/37.3.259.

3 Katrien Meert et al., "Taking a Shine to It: How the Preference for Glossy Stems from an Innate Need for Water," *Journal of Consumer Psychology* 24, no. 2 (April 2014): 195-206. See also Richard G. Coss et al., "All That Glistens: II. The Effects of Reflective Surface Finishes on the Mouthing Activity of Infants and Toddlers," *Ecological Psychology* 15, no. 3 (June 2010): 197-213.

4 Maria Sledmere, "Hypercritique: Toward a Lyric Architecture for the Anthropocene," Ph.D. dissertation in progress, University of Glasgow.

5 John Jarboe, email interview with the author, March 2, 2020.

6 Stallings, "Glitter," 49.

7 Peppa Pig, "School Project," Episode 10, Season 5, created by Astley Baker Davies Ltd. *Entertainment One*, originally aired June 26, 2017.

8 Peppa Pig, "Masks," Episode 24, Season 5, created by Astley Baker Davies Ltd. *Entertainment One*, originally aired September 5, 2017.

9 *Spies in Disguise*, directed by Nick Bruno and Troy Quane (December 25, 2019), 20th Century Fox, DVD.

10 The *Trolls* franchise also features many rainbow color schemes, including the logo for *Trolls World Tour*. Rainbows and rainbow color schemes, as discussed throughout this book, are often but not exclusively associated with LGBTQ+ communities.

11 *Trolls World Tour*, directed by Walt Dohrn (April 10, 2020), DreamWorks Animation, DVD.

12 White, "Never Cleaning Up," 167.

13 I should also note here that the film features many queer moments. When Lance returns to the agency office, he fistbumps a starstruck male staffer. The staffer's male coworker quips, "Never wash that hand again"—and then asks, "Can I hold it?" "Yeah!" the staffer responds. *Spies* also features a subplot wherein Lance's character gets turned into a female pigeon who lays an egg.

14 This narrative mirrors another children's book, Stella J. Jones' *Glitter* from 2017, in which Gloria the rhino antagonizes her fellow townsfolk by spreading glitter everywhere.

15 Ian Failes, "How DreamWorks Solved Troll Glitter," *befores & afters*, April 11, 2020, https://beforesandafters.com/2020/04/11/how-dreamworks-solved-glitter-for-trolls-world-tour/.

16 Youxi Woo, personal communication with the author (Google doc), June 22+, 2021.

17 Woo, personal communication.

18 Woo, personal communication.

19 Failes, "How DreamWorks Solved Troll Glitter," *befores & afters*.

20 Woo, Zoom interview with the author.

21 Youxi Woo and Doug Rizeakos, "Trolls World Tour: Desert Bling," abstract for SIGGRAPH conference presentation, August 9-13, 2021.

22 Nicole Starosielski, "'Movements That Are Drawn: A History of Environmental Animation from *The Lorax* to *Fern Gully* to *Avatar*." *The International Communication Gazette* 73, no. 1–2 (2011): 148.

23 *120 BPM*, directed by Robin Campillo, Memento Films, 2017.

24 Amy Michaels, *Facebook* post, December 15, 2019, https://www.facebook.com/amymichaelsmusic/photos/a .572585689424642/3233895419960309/?type=3&comment_id =3237075759642275.

25 Ren Ellis Neyra, "Queer Poetics," *Cambridge Companion to Queer Studies*, ed. Siobhan Somerville (Cambridge: Cambridge University Press, 2020), 125-141. Interestingly, "vibraphonic," like "bling," is a made-up word that nonetheless captures the pleasure and animacy of the latter term. And Thompson, *Shine*, 24-25, quoting Lee Bok's *The Little Book of Bling!* (Bath: Crombie Jardine Publishing Limited, 2005).

26 "Glitter Trolls," https://adampidia.fandom.com/wiki/Misc. _Trolls#Glitter_Trolls.

27 See http://www.cinemasoapbox.net/movie/emmas-review-of -trolls or https://www.scarymommy.com/universal-orlando -guy-diamond-glitter-fart/.

28 Taylor Pittman, "A Stunning, Glittery Look at The Impossible Beauty Standards Women Face," *Huffington Post*, February 19, 2015, https://www.huffingtonpost.co.uk/entry/hannah-altman -glitter-photos_n_6715708?ri18n=true.

29 Keith Gibson, "Hey Graduates, Get the Picture: Glitter is Litter," *FGCU 360*, December 2, 2019, https://fgcu360.com /2019/12/02/hey-graduates-get-the-picture-glitter-is-litter/.

30 See https://www.nytimes.com/2020/04/15/parenting/kids -potty-humor.html.

31 Nathan Reese, "Someone in Brooklyn is Covering Dog Poop with Glitter," *Complex*, May 19, 2014, https://www.complex .com/pop-culture/2014/05/someone-in-brooklyn-is-covering -dog-poop-with-glitter.

32 Caity Weaver, "What is Glitter?", *The New York Times*, December 21, 2018, https://www.nytimes.com/2018/12/21/style/glitter-factory.html.

33 See https://www.reddit.com/r/UnresolvedMysteries/comments/a8hrk0/which_mystery_industry_is_the_largest_buyer_of/. See also https://www.wbur.org/endlessthread/2019/11/08/the-great-glitter-mystery, which seems to have solved the mystery: glitter is used in coating boats, waterskis, and other water leisure industry materials.

34 Parisa Ahmadi, "Perils and Possibilities of Enchantment: Glitter as a Case Study," seminar paper for Dr. Noah Tamarkin, April 24, 2019.

35 Bob Blackledge proves useful here again: "Glitter particles are usually so small that it is not intended that an observer will be able to discern a shape"—which are usually hexagonal, square, or rectangular—"they only see a flash of reflected light." Blackledge, "GLITTER as Forensic Evidence," 7.

36 "Bedazzle"—an intransitive verb invented by Shakespeare— functions similarly. *Merriam-Webster* offers the definitions, "to confuse by a strong light" and "to impress forcefully." Centuries later, NSI Innovations introduced The BeDazzler, a home craft machine that adds glitter's distant cousins, rhinestones, to articles of clothing.

37 See https://www.dsl.ac.uk/entry/snd/glamsy.

38 In this film, the pieces of "glitter" in question measure up to 2 inches long, much like those in *120 BPM*; some might therefore describe it instead as confetti. Wikipedia claims that "glitter is smaller than confetti (pieces usually no larger than 1mm [.039 inches]) and is universally shiny," whereas confetti is larger and often made of paper. See https://en.wikipedia.org/wiki/Confetti. However, given that the Mariah Carey film refers to this larger substance as "glitter," we could say that there is some significant slippage between the two terms.

39 See Maya Allen, "A Speck of Glitter Caused This Woman to Lose Her Eye," *Cosmopolitan*, April 7, 2016, https://www.cosmopolitan.com/style-beauty/beauty/news/a56476/woman-loses-eye-from-glitter/. And Press Association, "Woman Nearly Blinded by Christmas Card Glitter," *The Guardian*, January 2, 2018, https://www.theguardian.com/society/2018/jan/02/woman-nearly-blinded-by-christmas-card-glitter.

40 "Matter of Amato v. R.R. Heywood Co., Inc.," *CaseText*, https://casetext.com/case/matter-of-amato-v-rr-heywood-co-inc-1.

41 White, "Never Cleaning Up," 178.

42 "Trashion Visual Artist Series: Machine Dazzle," Sonoma Community Center, https://sonomacommunitycenter.org/trashion-virtual-artist-series-machine-dazzle/.

Chapter 4

1 Admittedly, though, alternate terms exist: the United States Food and Drug Administration notes that "many decorative glitters and dusts are sold over the Internet and in craft and bakery supply stores under names such as luster dust, disco dust, twinkle dust, sparkle dust, highlighter, shimmer powder, pearl dust, and petal dust." "FDA Advises Home and Commercial Bakers to Avoid Use of Non-Edible Food Decorative Products," US Food and Drug Administration, January 14, 2018, https://www.fda.gov/food/food-additives-petitions/fda-advises-home-and-commercial-bakers-avoid-use-non-edible-food-decorative-products.

2   Debbie Chapman, "How to Make Homemade Glitter," *One Little Project*, July 25, 2016, https://onelittleproject.com/homemade-glitter/.

3   Amanda Boetzkes, *Plastic Capitalism: Contemporary Art and the Drive to Waste* (Cambridge: The MIT Press, 2019), 182.

4   Leddy, "Sparkle and Shine," 260. And Madison Roberts, "These Outrageous Sparkly Foods Are Made with Edible Glitter—Here Are All the Places You Can Eat Them," *People*, April 6, 2018, https://people.com/food/edible-glitter-foods/.

5   "Glitter Gravy! By Popaball," Popaball Ltd., YouTube Video, 0:36, November 22, 2018, https://www.youtube.com/watch?v=aBovjZ0eUwM.

6   Dagwoods (@dagwoodspizza), "Coming Back Again Soon by Popular Demand; the #magicalAF Edible Glitter Pizza!!!!," Instagram photo, April 9, 2018, https://www.instagram.com/p/BhXiZGfBQQ5/?utm_source=DesignTAXI&utm_medium=DesignTAXI&utm_term=DesignTAXI&utm_content=DesignTAXI&utm_campaign=DesignTAXI.

7   Alice Fisher, "Why the Unicorn Has Become the Emblem for Our Times," *The Guardian*, October 15, 2017, https://www.theguardian.com/society/2017/oct/15/return-of-the-unicorn-the-magical-beast-of-our-times.

8   Jennifer Ladino, *Memorials Matter: Affect and Environment at American Memory Sites* (Reno: University of Nevada Press, 2019), 81.

9   Stephanie Breijo, "We've Gone Too Far: Now You Can Get Glitter Pizza in Santa Monica," *TimeOut*, June 20, 2018, https://www.timeout.com/los-angeles/news/weve-gone-too-far-now-you-can-get-glitter-pizza-in-santa-monica-062018.

10 Adolph Loos, "Ornament and Crime," *Programs and Manifestos on 20th-Century Architecture*, ed. Ulrich Conrads, trans. Michael Bullock (Cambridge: The MIT Press, 1971), 20.

11 Consumer Reports, "You're Literally Eating Microplastics. How You Can Cut Down Exposure to Them," *The Washington Post*, October 7, 2019, https://www.washingtonpost.com/health/youre-literally-eating-microplastics-how-you-can-cut-down-exposure-to-them/2019/10/04/22ebdfb6-e17a-11e9-8dc8-498eabc129a0_story.html.

12 Rachel Wearmouth, "Durham Businesswoman Left with £18k Legal Bill after Selling 'Edible' Cupcake Glitter with Plastic Shavings in It," *Chronicle Live*, April 26, 2014, https://www.chroniclelive.co.uk/news/north-east-news/durham-businesswoman-left-18k-legal-7010652.

13 Kendall Jones, "Seattle Breweries Are Celebrating Pride Week with Glitter Beer," *Seattle Magazine*, November 27, 2018, https://www.seattlemag.com/eat-and-drink/seattle-breweries-are-celebrating-pride-week-glitter-beer.

14 "Bad Ideas in Brewing—Glitter Beer," *American Craft Beer* blog, March 5, 2018, https://www.americancraftbeer.com/bad-ideas-brewing-glitter-beer/#:~:text=Glitter%20is%20similar%20to%20confetti,making%20its%20way%20into%20beer.

15 Jeff Alworth, "Glitter Beer: The Full Report," *Beervana* blog, March 20, 2018, https://www.beervanablog.com/beervana/2018/3/19/glitter-beer-the-full-report.

16 Senga Green, et al., "All That Glitters Is Litter?", 2.

17 "Credentials," *Bioglitter.com*, 2018, https://www.bioglitter.com/cosmetic-bioglitter/credentials/.

18 Trashyreece, "What Do You All Think about the 'Tea' on Trixie Cosmetics?," *Reddit*, May 30, 2019, https://www.reddit.com/r/rupaulsdragrace/comments/buuwf4/what_do_you_all_think_about_the_tea_on_trixie/. (But maybe drag queens who use plastic containers for their low-plastic glitters shouldn't throw rocks . . .)

19 "What Are the Benefits of Pura Products?," *Purabioglitter.com*, 2020, https://www.purabioglitter.com.br/faq.

20 See https://www.purabioglitter.com.br/compras-no-atacado, https://www.culturehustleusa.com/collections/powders/products/dazzle-the-worlds-glitteriest-plant-based-eco-glitter-pack-5-x-10g, and https://ecostardust.com/apps/help-center#hc-why-is-there-still-a-plastic-window-in-my-tin.

21 Senga Green et. al, "All That Glitters is Litter?," 6.

22 de Araújo, "Shimmery Waste," 2.

23 Senga Green et. al, "All That Glitters is Litter?," 5. Ironically, then, pollution actually helps some creatures thrive, as the authors note. The aim of this study was not to test the actual biogradability *of* glitters marketed as biodegradable, but rather to test their potential ecological impacts.

24 Brando Baranzelli, "Behind the Glitter: Mica and Child Mining in India," *Al Jazeera* video, 25:00, June 12, 2020, https://www.aljazeera.com/program/101-east/2020/6/12/behind-the-glitter-mica-and-child-mining-in-india/.

25 "Modern Slavery Statement 2019/2020," *Lush*, December 31, 2020, https://weare.lush.com/lush-life/our-policies/modern-slavery-statement/. "The Lush Ethical Charter," *Lush*, April 29, 2020, https://weare.lush.com/lush-life/our-ethics/the-lush-ethical-charter/.

26 Malin Ah-King and Eva Hayward, "Toxic Sexes: Perverting Pollution and Queering Hormone Disruption," *O-Zone: A Journal of Object-Oriented Studies* no. 1 (2013): 5. See also Alexis Shotwell's book *Against Purity: Living Ethically in Compromised Times* (Minneapolis: University of Minnesota Press, 2016).

27 Jenny Price, *Stop Saving the Planet! An Environmentalist Manifesto* (New York: W. W. Norton & Company, 2021), 13–22.

28 Low, Zoom correspondence with the author.

29 Susan Stewart, *Painted Faces: A Colourful History of Cosmetics* (Gloucestershire: Amberley Publishing, 2017), 16. And Joshua Hammer, "Only a Handful of People Can Enter the Chauvet Cave Each Year. Our Reporter Was One of Them," *Smithsonian Magazine*, April 14, 2015, https://www.smithsonianmag.com /arts-culture/only-handful-people-can-enter-chauvet-cave -each-year-our-reporter-was-one-them-180954981/.

30 "A History of the World—Object: Cosmetic Palette," *BBC*, 2014, http://www.bbc.co.uk/ahistoryoftheworld/objects/s -OMbtkESJ6aV6_k6o86oA. See also Aileen Ribeiro, *Facing Beauty: Painted Women and Cosmetic Art* (New Haven: Yale University Press, 2011), 38.

31 Amy Breau, "Why Did Cleopatra Wear Makeup?," *Indiana Public Media*, August 31, 2012, https://indianapublicmedia .org/amomentofscience/cleopatra-wear-makeup.php.

32 Peter Roger Stuart Moorey, *Ancient Mesopotamian Materials and Industries: The Archaeological Evidence* (State College, PA: Pennsylvania State University Press, 1999), 86.

33 Having interviewed multiple archaeologists and museum curators, author Chris Barton confirms in his forthcoming children's book *Glitter Everywhere* (Watertown: Charlesbridge

Publishing, 2022) that there is no existing evidence for the crushed-beetle claim.

34 Ribeiro, *Facing Beauty,* 273.

35 Robert Southey, "The Cataract of Lodore," *Poetry Foundation,* https://www.poetryfoundation.org/poems/57951/the-cataract-of-lodore.

36 Deborah Bird Rose "Shimmer: When All You Love Is Being Trashed," in *Arts of Living on a Damaged Planet: Ghosts and Monsters of the Anthropocene,* ed. Anna Lowenhaupt Tsing, et al. (Minneapolis: University of Minnesota Press, 2017), G53.

37 Eddy Francisco Alvarez Jr., "Finding Sequins in the Rubble: Stitching Together an Archive of Trans Latina Los Angeles," *Transgender Studies Quarterly* 3, no. 3-4 (November 2016): 622. Alvarez is drawing on conversations with designer Luz Espinoza.

38 Adams Media Corporation, *Glitter!: A Celebration of Sparkle* (New York: Simon & Schuster, 2018).

39 Online Etymology Dictionary, "glitter (n.)," https://www.etymonline.com/word/glitter.

40 Curtis Honeycutt, "Grammar Guy: May I Have a Word," *Bennington Banner,* July 4, 2021, https://www.benningtonbanner.com/curtis-honeycutt-grammar-guy-may-i-have-a-word/article_b4cbe80a-db37-11eb-9617-13da07be0e49.html.

41 While 1970s glam or glitter rock certainly had queer undertones, glitter as a product/object was not explicitly marketed at this time to LGBTQ+ communities; the latter were not perceived as lucrative consumer bases until the 1990s.

42 Jeena Sharma, "This Short Film Imagines a Sustainable, Glitter-Filled Universe," *Paper*, April 22, 2019, https://www.papermag.com/bioglitz-short-film-earth-day-2635263914.html?rebelltitem=4#rebelltitem4.

43 "lanalabia," Instagram profile, https://www.instagram.com/lanalabia/?hl=en. See also https://www.instagram.com/p/CFy8E_NKDVk/?utm_source=ig_web_copy_link.

44 See https://www.instagram.com/BioGlitz/.

45 Tomasz W. Kozlowski (@TomaszTweets), "You'd think it would be getting better, but it's not . . . Pictures from last year below (Whitehall and Trafalgar Square)," Tweet, July 8, 2019, https://twitter.com/TomaszTweets/status/1148203527925325824.

46 "Plastic Free Pride," *OUT for Sustainability*, https://out4s.org/plasticfreepride/. On the origins of the flag colors, see https://gilbertbaker.com/rainblow-flag-color-meanings/.

47 Lynn Segerblom, "The Woman Behind the Rainbow Flag," *Los Angeles Blade*, March 2, 2018, https://www.losangelesblade.com/2018/03/02/woman-behind-rainbow-flag/.

48 Kate Soper, "Alternative Hedonism, Cultural Theory and the Role of Aesthetic Revisioning," *Cultural Studies* 22, no. 5 (September 2018): 571, 578.

49 Kate Soper, "A New Hedonism: A Post-Consumerism Vision," *The Next System Project*, November 22, 2017, 22, https://thenextsystem.org/learn/stories/new-hedonism-post-consumerism-vision#consumerism-and-its-discontents.

50 "EcoStardust Biodegradable Glitter Pure," *EcoStardust*, https://ecostardust.com/collections/ecostardust-biodegradable-glitter-pure.

51 Jocelyn Read, email correspondence with the author, May 7, 2021. For more information on the physics of glitter, see: https://www.discoverbioglitter.com/bioglitter_physics_of_light/#:~:text=Opalescent%20and%20Iridescent%20glitters%20utilise,spun%20back%20on%20itself%20back. And "Glitter Colour Effects and The Bioglitter Equivalents," *Bioglitter. com*, November 5, 2020, https://www.discoverbioglitter.com /bioglitter_physics_of_light/#:~:text=Opalescent%20and% 20Iridescent%20glitters%20utilise,spun%20back%20on%20it self%20back.

52 "FAQ on Lush and Mica," *Lush*, https://www.lushusa.com/ stories/article_faq-lush-and-mica.html.

53 "All That Glitters . . .", *Lush*, https://www.lush.com/uk/en/a/all -glitters.

54 See https://www.facebook.com/purabioglitter/about/?referrer =services_landing_page.

55 Gay Hawkins, "Plastic Bags: Living with Rubbish," *International Journal of Cultural Studies* 4, no. 1 (March 2001): 9.

56 "Connecting People and the Planet with Glitter," *Projekt Glitter*, https://projektglitter.com/mission.

57 Jill Dolan, *Geographies of Learning: Theory and Practice, Activism and Performance* (Middletown: Wesleyan University Press, 2001), 99.

58 Andrei S. Markovits and Joseph Klaver, "Alive and Well into the Fourth Decade of Their Bundestag Presence: A Tally of the Greens' Impact on the Federal Republic of Germany's Political Life and Public Culture," *German Politics and Society* 33, no. 4 (2015): 112-140. See also Stephen Milder's *Greening Democracy: The Anti-Nuclear Movement and Political*

Environmentalism in West Germany and Beyond, 1968-1983
(Cambridge: Cambridge University Press), 2017.

59 "EQNM Queer Beer with Glitter," *Untappd* reviews, https://
untappd.com/b/tractor-brewing-co-eqnm-queer-beer-with
-glitter/2667963.

60 "Celebrate Pride Month with Elysian's GLITTERis Pride Ale,"
National Distributors, June 13, 2019, https://www.nat-dist
.com/2019/06/13/celebrate-pride-month-with-elysian-glitteris
-pride-ale/.

61 "Elysian Brewing, the Queer Eye Guy, and Glitter Beer,"
American Craft Beer blog, May 2, 2019, https://www.
americancraftbeer.com/elysian-brewingthe-queer-eye-guy
-and-glitter-beer/.

62 Like other glitter-loving artists such as Grandma Moses,
Fontana's work was considered vulgar at the time. Today,
their work commands millions at auction. Lucio Fontana,
Concetto Spaziale, 1957, oil, sand, and glitter on canvas, Peggy
Guggenheim Collection, Venice, https://www.guggenheim
-venice.it/en/art/works/concetto-spaziale-2/.

63 Jeff Alworth, "Glitter Beer," https://www.beervanablog.com/
beervana/2018/3/19/glitter-beer-the-full-report.

Chapter 5

1 Stallings, "Glitter," 49.

2 Moore with Phillips, *Plastic Ocean*, 328, 107.

3 Linsey E. Haram, et al., "A Plasticene Lexicon," *Marine
Pollution Bulletin* 150 (January 2020), 2. Haram et al. trace the

use of the term "Plasticene" to paleoclimatologist Curtis Stager in 2011, who was riffing on blogger Matt Dowling.

4 Haram, et al., "A Plasticene Lexicon," 3.

5 David Farrier, *Footprints: In Search of Future Fossils* (New York: Farrar, Straus, & Giroux, 2020).

6 Moore with Phillips, *Plastic Ocean*, 117.

7 Timothy Clark, *Ecocriticism on the Edge: The Anthropocene as a Threshold Concept* (London: Bloomsbury Academic, 2015), 72.

8 Max Liboiron, "Waste Colonialism," *Discard Studies*, November 1, 2018, https://discardstudies.com/2018/11/01/waste-colonialism/. Scholars of waste colonialism and environmental (in)justice have noted, for example, that dumps and incinerators are typically sited in poor neighborhoods. Meanwhile, waste from the Global North is often shipped off to the Global South.

9 Margaret Ronda, "Obsolesce," in *Veer Ecology: A Companion for Environmental Thinking*, ed. Jeffrey Jerome Cohen and Lowell Duckert (Minneapolis: University of Minnesota Press, 2017), 78. Here, Ronda is quoting Michael Thompson's 1979 anthropological survey of waste, *Rubbish Theory*. I wish to acknowledge that Thompson's use of the term "blindness" reads as insensitive from a disability standpoint.

10 "Municipal Solid Waste," Environmental Protection Agency, https://archive.epa.gov/epawaste/nonhaz/municipal/web/html/.

11 Katie Schaag, "The Pleasures of Teaching Plastic," *Edge Effects*, October 12, 2019, https://edgeeffects.net/teaching-plastic/.

12   Martin F. Manalansan IV, "The Messy Itineraries of Queerness," Society for Cultural Anthropology Editor's Forum, July 21, 2015, https://culanth.org/fieldsights/the-messy-itineraries-of-queerness.

13   Eleanor Cummins, "Guys, Glitter is Not the Real Enemy Here," *Slate*, December 1, 2017, https://slate.com/technology/2017/12/the-proposed-global-ban-on-glitter-is-pointless.html.

14   Heather Davis, "Toxic Progeny: The Plastiphere and Other Queer Futures," *philoSOPHIA* 5, no. 2 (2015): 231.

15   Hannah Klaubert, "Welcome to the Queer Plastisphere: Heather Davis," *Sonic Acts*, https://sonicacts.com/mobile/critical/welcome-to-the-queer-plastisphere-heather-davis.

16   Alexander S. Tagg and Juliana A. Ivar do Sul, "Is This Your Glitter? An Overlooked But Potentially Environmentally-Valuable Microplastic," *Marine Pollution Bulletin* 146 (September 2019), 51.

17   First two quotations, Coleman, *Glitterworlds*, 18, 23. Third quotation, Weaver, "What is Glitter?"

18   Recall Krista Thompson's point about how the cultural practices of urban African diasporic communities—such as the wearing of "bling"—"disrupt notions of value by privileging not things but their visual effects." Thompson, *Shine*, 25.

19   Low, Zoom correspondence with the author. I'm indebted to Christine Harold's *Things Worth Keeping: The Value of Attachment in a Disposable World* (Minneapolis: University of Minnesota Press, 2020) for introducing me to this concept of "opening up" objects.

20 "Bad Ideas In Brewing—Glitter Beer," https://www
.americancraftbeer.com/bad-ideas-brewing-glitter-beer/.

21 On the connection between waste and taste, see Guy Schaffer,
"Queering Waste through Camp," *Discard Studies*, February
2015, https://discardstudies.com/2015/02/27/queering-waste
-through-camp/.

22 "Glitterology: Is Glitter a Color?," https://glitterology.weebly.com/.

23 "Julio Torres Stand-Up," Youtube video, 05:32, April 27, 2018,
https://www.youtube.com/watch?v=9s7U51XQfhc&t=173s.

24 Jonathan Hogeback, "Are Black and White Colors?",
Brittanica, https://www.britannica.com/story/are-black-and
-white-colors.

25 *Velvet Goldmine*.

26 Ellen Meloy, *The Last Cheater's Waltz: Beauty and Violence in
the Desert Southwest* (New York: Henry Holt and Company,
2014), 11.

27 Jennifer A. Wagner-Lawlor, "Plastic's 'Untiring Solicitation':
Geographies of Myth, Corporate Alibis, and the Plaesthetics
of the Matacão," *Life in Plastic: Artistic Responses to
Petromodernity*, ed. Caren Irr (Minneapolis: University of
Minnesota Press, 2021), 263.

28 Leddy, "Sparkle and Shine," 271.

29 Rose, "Shimmer," G53.

30 Bonnie Burton, "Newly Discovered 'Glitter Worms' Dance
and Fight One Another Underwater," *CNET*, May 14, 2020,
https://www.cnet.com/news/scientists-discover-new-colorful
-glitter-fighting-worms-living-deep-underwater/.

31 Burton, "Newly Discovered."

32 Olivia Parkes, "You Can Literally Have Sex with the Environment in This 'Ecosexual Bathhouse,'" *Vice*, June 5, 2016, https://www.vice.com/en/article/d7anjq/you-can-literally-have-sex-with-the-environment-in-this-ecosexual-bathhouse.

33 Käte Hamburger Centre for Apocalyptic and Postapocalyptic Studies (CAPAS), https://boku.ac.at/fileadmin/data/themen/Zentrum_fuer_Umweltgeschichte/News/2021_News/Brosch_CAPAS_2.pdf.

INDEX